The Karakoram Highway and the Hunza Valley, 1998

History, Culture, Experiences

Annette Bräker and
Horst H. Geerken

(Compiled by Horst H. Geerken)

A BukitCinta Book

Bibliografische Information der Deutschen Bibliothek:
Die Deutsche Bibliothek verzeichnet diese Publikation in der
Deutschen Nationalbibliografie; detaillierte bibliografische
Daten sind im Internet über http://dnb.dbd.de abrufbar.

© 2017 Horst H. Geerken, 53177 Bonn

German Original Title: Der Karakorum Highway und das Hunzatal, 1998
Cover Design and Maps: Sabine Berner-Hoffmann
All photographs unless otherwise attributed ©Horst H. Geerken
Editors of the German Edition: Michaela Mattern and Barbara Bode
Editors of the English Edition: Dilys McCann, Horst H. Geerken and Barbara Bode
Layout & Design: Barbara Bode
Typeset in Adobe Garamond Pro
Production and Publication: BoD - Books on Demand, Norderstedt
Printed in Germany

ISBN 978-3-7448-1279-5

The Karakoram Highway and the Hunza Valley, 1998
History, Culture, Experiences

Annette Bräker and
Horst H. Geerken
(Compiled by Horst H. Geerken)

Translated by Bill McCann

A BukitCinta Book

In memory of Annette's and my parents,
wonderful people, who always supported
and encouraged our travels to the Orient,
even in our youth. They awakened our love
for travel and other cultures,
for which we thank them.
(Horst H. Geerken)

Contents

1. Foreword Horst H. Geerken, 2016 7
2. Foreword Annette Bräker, 1998 15
3. Arrival in Islamabad 16
4. From Islamabad to Gilgit on the Karakoram Highway 19
5. Into the Hunza Valley from Gilgit to Karimabad 44
6. The Hopar Valley 78
7. From Karimabad to Gulmit 84
8. From Gulmit to Sust 98
9. From Sust over the Khunjerab Pass to Kashgar 102
10. Xinjiang 124
11. The Kashgar Oasis 127
12. The Return Journey to the Hunza Valley 151
13. The First Westerners to Visit the Hunza Valley 193
14. To Islamabad and Lahore 203
15. Back to Germany 217
16. The Karakoram Highway and the Hunza Valley 2015/2016 .. 219
17. Thanks 223
18. Literature 226
19. Index of Persons 228
20. Subject Index 230

Ill. 1: Our route

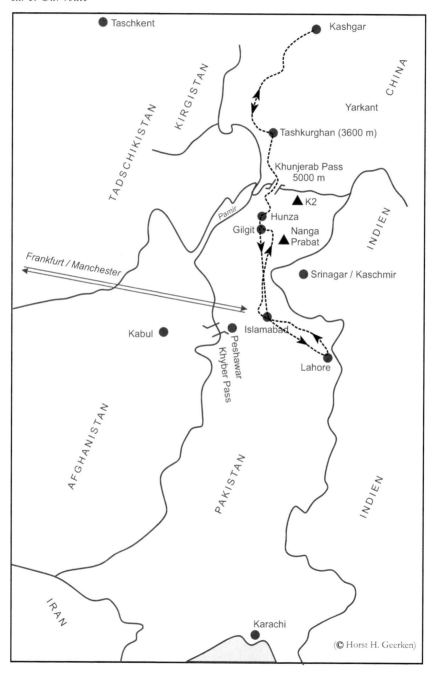

1. Foreword
Horst H. Geerken

The Hunza Valley and its secondary valleys lie in an extremely inaccessible area of the Hindu Kush. It is a high valley – between 2,500 and 3,500 metres high between the Karakoram and Hindu Kush ranges –, surrounded by 7,000-metre peaks, of which Rakaposhi is the highest at around 7,800 metres.

Herodotus (about 450 B.C.) was the first author to mention this region, bordering on Kashmir and close to Afghanistan.[1] Dr Gottlieb[2] Wilhelm Leitner, an orientalist and linguist who was born in Hungary[3] in 1840 and died in 1899 in Bonn, was the first scientist to visit the Hunza Valley, among other regions in the Hindu Kush, in the 1860s and 1880s. His books about the history, languages, religions, customs, legends and songs of the region are interesting and important works of reference even today.

The paths along the steep mountainsides in the impassable terrain along the river Hunza and the simple suspended bridges were so narrow, that goods could only be carried by porters on most stretches of the way. As the Hunzakuts[4] say, a rider here has to carry his horse!

The main language spoken in the Hunza Valley is the isolated Burushaski. The influence of Greece resulting from Alexander the Great's invasion around 325 B.C. is still evident today in sculptures and the genetic (European and Aryan) characteristics of the Hunzakut. You often see blond hair or blue eyes, which are not typical of Pakistan. The inhabitants of the Hunza Valley regard themselves as descendants of the warrior king Alexander the Great and his army. Many of Alexander's warriors did not wish to undertake the difficult return journey to their homeland and exchanged the sword for the ploughshare. Alexander founded villages and towns in the Indus and Hunza Valleys and settled his Greek and Macedonian veterans there. He encouraged marriage with the local women. The language, music and dances resemble those of Macedonia and Albania even today. In the almost inaccessible Hunza region it was possible for the genetic and cultural characteristics of the invaders to survive almost undiluted. According to legend, the King of Hunza is said to be a direct descendant of Alexander the Great. The founder of the dynasty was called King Alexander Iskandar Shah. Outside the Hunza Valley Alexander's soldiers also founded city states, but these resulted in more mixed cultures.

---

1 Herodotus, *III.* p. 102-105 und *IV.* p. 13-27
2 In many British publications also called Georg
3 Many British publications also give Austria as his birthplace, since the area belonged to Austria-Hungary at the time
4 or Hunza people

Because of its isolated position, it was easy to defend the Hunza Valley against invaders, which is why the Hunzakuts managed to live there largely independent and free of foreign influence for about 1,000 years. In 1889 Britain attempted to conquer the Hunza Valley, only finally succeeding in 1892. Mir[5] Safdar Ali, the King of the Hunzakuts, had fled shortly before to China. As Durand writes in his book[6], the British treated the Mir very badly. They took his kingdom away from him without giving him any chance to negotiate, in spite of several attempts on his part. He died impoverished in exile in Xinjiang in 1930.[7]

From 1892 to 1947 the Hunza Valley was administered by the British as part of British India. Just as India and Pakistan took over the British mandate in Hunza after the Second World War, Britain took over the Chinese mandate in 1892.

When the British withdrew from the Hunza Valley in 1947 – after independence and the partition of the former British colony of India into Hindu India and Muslim Pakistan –, it aroused India's covetousness. India tried to retain control of Gilgit and Hunza and began an inexcusable war. The mountain people of the Hunza Valley fought the aggressors off successfully and prevented their annexation. In the great park in Gilgit stands a monument, the "Minaret of the Martyrs", a memorial to this war, which remained totally unknown in the West.

In 1947 the kingdom was abolished by the British. The former ruler and his descendants were allowed to retain the title of "Mir" as a symbol of respect, as well as the red number plates with 'Hunza 1' and 'Hunza 2' on their cars in gold lettering. In the years that followed, foreign visitors were not allowed to enter the area. Only in 1974 was the Hunza Valley incorporated into the Gilgit-Baltistan region under the Pakistani central government, and visits by foreigners to the lower part of the valley were permitted.

Until 1950 the children of the Hunzakuts had not seen a bicycle or a motor vehicle. All goods, like tools, cooking utensils, oil lamps, mirrors and other glassware, nails and building materials – in fact, nearly everything needed for everyday life – had to be carried into the valley on the backs of porters.

The mountainous terrain has only a few level areas which can be used for agricultural purposes such as growing corn, apricots and grapes. Pastoral farming is restricted to goats and poultry – mainly ducks. The indigenous population's diet is almost entirely meatless. Even dairy products such as milk, butter and cheese are

---

5 "Mir" was the ruler's title.
6 Algernon George Arnold Durand, *The Making of a Frontier: Five Years of Experiences and Adventures in Gilgit, Hunza, Nagar, Chitral and the Eastern Hindu-Kush*, 1900
7 Historically East Turkestan or Chinese Turkestan

not consumed very often. The legendary longevity and good health of the Hunzakuts is mainly attributed to the glacier water, its milky appearance due to the rich admixture of minerals and noble metals, and to their diet of mainly wholemeal foods. Men well over 100 years of age, who still farm their own fields or play polo, are no rarity. For this reason the Hunza Valley, which is often considered to be the lost kingdom of Shangri La[8], is also called the "Oasis of Eternal Youth".

The women in the Hunza Valley, with their brightly coloured caps under a white veil, are self-confident and totally free. Their faces are open, and they are always prepared to smile. Unlike the surrounding Islamic areas, monogamy is the rule here, and both partners have to agree to enter a marriage. No distinction is made between men and women. Even on her wedding night, a woman can refuse her husband, and she has the right to be divorced. Today, in 2016, the Hunza Valley has about 90,000 inhabitants. At the time of our trip there were considerably fewer.

For many years the Hunza Valley was a forbidden realm for foreigners. In the south, it borders on Pakistan, in the north east on the Chinese autonomous province of Xinjiang, and in the north west on Afghanistan. It was only in 1974 that the news that "the Hunza Valley is now open" rang out to the world. But why were foreigners forbidden to visit the little kingdom of Hunza until then?

There was a treaty between Pakistan and China guaranteeing the security of Hunza by China. Since the Chinese intended to invest heavily in the Karakoram Highway, they did not want foreigners to be able to see their cards. China was particularly sensitive about Xinjiang at the time, even though the uncertain border between Pakistan and China in the northern Hunza Valley had been corrected and firmly established in 1963. After the mandate was transferred from Britain to Pakistan, China was prepared to accept that Hunza – which had previously long been a Chinese mandated territory – became Pakistani. China saw that it was in their interests to have a safe buffer state between themselves and their southern neighbour.

Hunza was a country without criminality, without police, without prisons and without an administration. There were no hotels, no newspapers, and no banks – and also no motor vehicles or petrol stations. Electricity was unknown. Since the Hunzakuts were a robustly healthy people, there were no doctors or chemists either. No one had to pay any tax.

In the mountains surrounding the Hunza Valley many foreign travellers, mainly climbers, had vanished without trace. The Pakistani Prime Minister

---

8   James Hilton, *The Lost Horizon*, ISBN 978-00-62113726

would have had to accept responsibility for every traveller who entered the valley. And even for the Pakistani government the kingdom was still somewhat alien and mysterious: Hunza was markedly different from the rest of Pakistan, and so the valley was closed to foreigners for a long time.

For my brother Hartmut, the news that the Hunza Valley was open was the signal that he should immediately fly from Kabul to Gilgit via Rawalpindi. He and his son Olaf, then six years old, were among the first foreign visitors in May 1974.[9] At the time, my brother was head of the Goethe Institute in Kabul, Afghanistan. His son Olaf was probably the youngest foreign visitor ever to travel to the Hunza Valley. In Gilgit, and especially at the border with the Hunza Valley, they were greeted with bouquets of flowers. Visitors from the West were still seen as something special and a great rarity.

To enter the state of Hunza, it was necessary at that time to get the permission of the Pakistani government and to go through border controls. On the road between Gilgit and Karimabad there was a table, about a metre and a half long, set diagonally across the narrow path, with one person incorporating both the customs and immigration officers. He was dressed in typical Hunza costume, with a long, wide-sleeved, brown, felt-like woollen coat and the native Hunza cap, the farshin, with its characteristic rolled edge. The women, on the other hand, are always brightly dressed and wear brightly embroidered caps.

The passport was stamped, and the first question from the immigration officer was, "Would you like a drink of wine?" Wine in strictly Islamic Pakistan? The Hunza Valley has a special status, since its inhabitants are tolerant Ismailites, whose religious leader is the Aga Khan. The official produced a full bottle, sealed with clay, and opened it carefully so that none of the clay could crumble into the wine. It was a brownish, naturally cloudy wine, but according to my brother it was quite drinkable.

---

9   The porcelain manufacturer and mountaineer Philip Rosenthal from Selb visited the Hunza Valley and Nanga Parbat as early as the 1960s. How was it possible for him to enter the forbidden territory at that time? He had invited his guide, Sarbaz Khan from Aliabad, to Germany. Within a single year the latter learned German and also the production of simple porcelain, which he took back to Hunza. Sarbaz Khan was certainly at that time the only Hunzakut who could speak German. In 1998 we, however, met several Hunzakuts who could speak some German, probably as a result of the tourist industry. The guides on the Fairy Meadow near Nanga Parbat told us that Philip Rosenthal set up a flag made of Rosenthal porcelain on a peak neighbouring Nanga Parbat. At first we could not believe it, but in Gulmit it was confirmed to us by Abdullah Baig, the owner of the Hunza Marco Polo Inn Hotel. I wonder if the porcelain flag is still flying up there on one of the high peaks.

*Ill. 2:
Hunza stamp in my brother Hartmut's passport,
dated May 27th, 1974*

The Chinese were still hard at work constructing the Karakoram Highway (KKH). Near Gilgit there was the first Chinese workers' settlement, housing thousands of Chinese workers. It was a typical Chinese camp with temporary huts and tents. It was possible to buy Chinese goods, there was a canteen, a bakery and a large vegetable garden. It was a hive of activity. The Hunzakuts called the camp the "Camp of Smiles" and it was totally self-sufficient. All the signs were in Chinese script, including those on the pathways between the huts and tents. Foreigners were forbidden to enter the camp. The gateway to the Hunza Valley lay beyond the camp. The Chinese workers in their bright blue overalls and baker-boy caps were shovelling and hacking along the breathtakingly steep cliffs. It was reminiscent of a disturbed nest of blue ants.

The way up to the Hunza Valley was still very difficult. In those days you could go no further than Karimabad and Baltit. During their entire stay in the valley Hartmut and Olaf were looked after by Mr German, the chief secretary of the last Mir of the Hunzakuts. They were his guests, because at that time there were no restaurants anywhere in the entire Hunza Valley. He housed them first in Mir Muhammad Jamal Khan's guest house in Karimabad, and then in an apartment – there were no hotels then, either. In honour of Hartmut and Olaf a sheep was slaughtered and there was a great feast attended by all the dignitaries of Karimabad.

At the time when my brother was in the Hunza Valley with his son, the Mir of Hunza was in Germany for medical treatment. It was quite a strange coincidence that the place where the Mir was being treated by a Professor Stuhlinger was in Starnberg, close to my brother's home. While the Mir was being treated in

Germany, the moon in the Hunza Valley had an unusually large corona, which the Hunzakuts interpreted as a good and positive sign that things would go well for the Mir in far-off Germany, and that he would soon recover.

Only two years later, in March 1976, Mir Muhammad Jamal Khan died in Karimabad. Many years before his shaman had prophesied his death on exactly that day. After the death of the Mir, who was so loved by his people, the shaman refused to look into the future anymore.

Mr German requested Hartmut in the name of the Mir to stay in the Hunza Valley and work as a teacher of German, English and French. The Mir was very concerned to improve the education of his people, although the illiteracy rate was even at that time less than four percent. The best rate in Pakistan! All children in the Hunza Valley receive compulsory education down to this day. All the schools are heavily supported financially by the Aga Khan Foundation.

As a teacher, Hartmut would be given the finest house in the Hunza Valley for himself and his family, but after serious consideration, he decided to carry on in the Goethe Institute. After about a week in Karimabad Mr German placed the Mir's Jeep, with its Hunza 2 number plate, at Hartmut's disposal for his return journey to Gilgit.

Only two years after my brother, Annette's father, the orientalist Professor Hans Bräker, visited the Hunza Valley in 1976 in the company of Professor Hans-Joachim Klimkeit. Bräker taught at the University of Trier and was the founder and Director in Chief of the Federal Institute for Asiatic and International Studies in Cologne. Klimkeit worked in comparative religion and Indology, which he had studied with the renowned Professor Helmuth von Glasenapp in Tübingen. At the time of the trip Klimkeit held the Chair of Comparative Religion at the University of Bonn. They only had a week, and wished to explore the Hunza Valley by bicycle. For reasons of time they were unable to reach Karimabad because of the very bad road conditions.

Later Klimkeit was the boss of the co-author of this book, Annette Bräker, at the University of Bonn. The stories told by her father and her boss about their experiences in the Hunza Valley gave Annette an intense desire to visit the region, which was also known to me because of my brother's visit. My old Pakistani fellow-student, Mohiuddin Biyabani, kept me sporadically informed about the progress of the work on the KKH, and so I developed a plan to surprise Annette by suggesting a trip to the Hunza Valley, thus fulfilling a dream we both shared.

Ill. 3:
The orientalist Professor Hans Bräker in conversation with the author

Kashgar was intended to be the final destination of our journey. It is in western China in the province of Xinjiang,[10] which has a population of about 22 million, a surface area of over 17 percent of the Republic of China and is bordered by India, Pakistan, Afghanistan, Tajikistan, Kirgizstan, Kazakhstan, Russia, Tibet and Mongolia. With so many nations on its borders, it is not surprising that this area, called the Pamir Knot, gave rise to acquisitive desires on the part of the Western powers in both world wars on account of its outstanding strategic position. The diplomatic conflicts connected with the area, particularly between Britain and Russia, were called with some cynicism by the British "The Great Game".

In this book there is no space to deal with the Great Game except in a superficial manner. However, there are countless works dealing with the subject, especially in British literature, though the reports contained in the latter about the political game and the military encounters are of course depicted from a British viewpoint. In this book we wish to focus on cultural matters and the early exploration of the region.

---

10 Historically East Turkestan or Chinese Turkestan

Our journey from Gilgit through the Hunza Valley and Xinjiang to Kashgar was a unique – and at times quite adventurous – experience in a region of great interest in terms of both history and landscape. A journey like this is always unforgettable.

Horst H. Geerken
Autumn/Winter 2016/17

Ill. 4:
"The Great Game": a native is threatened by the Russian bear and the British lion.[11]

---

11 Cartoon from *Punch*, November 30th 1878, Wikipedia Public Domain

2. Foreword
Annette Bräker

This journey was a long-cherished wish, which came to fulfillment for us in 1998. Long before I heard of the Kingdom of Hunza, I was fascinated by the name Gilgit and the political controversies between the colonial powers of Britain and Russia connected with it – and also China – in what was called the "Great Game"! I absolutely had to go there, and began to take an interest in it. I quickly came across the legendary Kingdom of Hunza and its role in that "Great Game" – as the British said – as well as the Karakoram Highway, the road that was built with the sacrifice of countless human lives, and leads from Islamabad in Pakistan to Kashgar in western China. The wish – now extended to include driving the length of the Karakoram Highway – would certainly have remained a dream if Horst had not had the same dream for even longer than I. Now he surprised me with his plan, which gradually took clearer shape. We met Hanne and Tonny Rosiny, who had lived in Pakistan a long time and had already made the journey. Tonny Rosiny was a diplomat and author, and had already published some books about Pakistan.[12] The Rosinys gave us valuable tips and addresses, which were to prove very useful on the spot.

Finally, at the end of April 1998, the dream came true. We packed and unpacked until we had reduced our baggage to such an extent that each of us had only a relatively modest rucksack, weighing – including books – less than ten kilograms. As usual I suffered from a kind of travel fever: I became more and more nervous every day and would in the end have preferred to cancel the trip. But all that was forgotten when we finally took off on a British Airways flight from Manchester to Islamabad on the 30th of April 1998.

We have compiled this record of our journey together from the letters and other reports we wrote on our travels. The sections written by Horst are printed in italics.

Annette Bräker
Summer 1998

---

[12] *Pakistan. Drei Hochkulturen am Indus: Harappa, Gandhara, die Moguln; Pakistan. Kunst; Pakistan. DuMont Reiseführer*

3. Arrival in Islamabad

We took off from Frankfurt only slightly late, and an hour and a half later we were in Manchester. On arriving there we immediately sought out a quiet spot near an out-of-the-way loo – after all, we had six hours to kill before our connecting flight. We stretched out on two benches and immediately sank into a deep sleep, but only after emptying two of the little bottles of wine that we had brought from the plane. The food on British Airways was admittedly quite Spartan, but they were all the more generous with the wine, which they served in 20 centilitre bottles – and so copiously that you could cram your pockets full of them. And so we went to sleep straight away in our quiet corner. We slept for three of our six hours in Manchester, and so the time "just flew past". When it was time to board our connecting flight to Islamabad, we waited until almost the last, because we had heard in Frankfurt that the flight was not fully booked. This meant that we could see which seats were unoccupied, and then we each spread out over a whole row of seats so that we would have a comfortable place to sleep. A couple, who were obviously German, clearly found this behaviour outrageous and shot sideways glares at us the whole time, which didn't bother us a bit as we lay comfortably stretched out.

95 percent of the passengers were Pakistanis, and that's what it looked like towards the end of the flight. Chaos, confusion, dirt, the toilets overflowing – and no one was worried. A gigantic, picturesque Afghan armed with a kind of St Peter's staff walked up and down the aisle every now and again, making the whole flight even more oriental. We spent the entire flight lying down relaxed and slept another four hours. By the end of the flight we had a good supply of forks and spoons in our baggage. You have to be ready for anything!

During the steward's announcement that importing alcohol into Pakistan was strictly prohibited, Horst had calmly stuffed several more bottles of the generously distributed wine into his hand luggage to join our bottle of whisky and another of Fernet Branca. And so we landed in Islamabad at six o'clock in the morning just as the muezzin just began to sound – well-rested and with our own private bar in our luggage. I was still a bit nervous, however, because of the alcohol content of our hand luggage.

From the outside, the airport looked as if it was in the process of being pulled down, while the inside was small, shabby and totally chaotic. But in spite of this impression everything then went very smoothly. In spite of long queues, we were through passport control in five minutes, and while Horst fished our luggage out of the equally chaotic seeming crowd of people around the conveyor belt, I looked around to see where we could most easily smuggle the demon drink into the country past the customs control. And I did find a place where there wasn't really an exit, but where people with not much luggage were constantly being let through. Horst thought we should hold up our passports in our hands to make a good impression. And then we should, without looking to either right or left, simply march through. And that's what happened: one minute later we had left it all behind us without meeting a single customs officer. Impudence had triumphed once again! The whole process had lasted 15 minutes in all.

We exchanged a little money and then we were sitting in the taxi – with me jammed between our rucksacks – on the way to the Ambassador Hotel. After what my mother and Rosiny had said, we were not expecting a great deal of the hotel, but we were pleasantly surprised. We're staying in what is presumably the same corner room where my parents stayed in 1983. The room is tidy and clean, like the whole hotel, at whose door stands a picturesquely costumed – or rather uniformed – doorman with a big rifle, who always pulls the door open devotedly, even when you don't want to go out.

Ill. 5:
The doorman

Although we had enthused to each other, after arriving here in Islamabad, about how pleasant it was to arrive at our destination rested, because we had been able to lie down on the plane and get sufficient sleep, we could hardly keep our eyes open after 10 o'clock in the morning, and every time between our "organisational trips" – travel agency, lunch, car hire, then travel agency again – we came even close to a bed, we simply fell in and fell into a deep sleep.

In the meantime we have slept another four hours here in the Ambassador Hotel, but in the active phases in between we've also sorted out everything necessary for our onward journey. Tomorrow morning at seven a hire car will pick us up here and drive us the two day journey along the Indus Valley to Gilgit. It was actually Horst who arranged everything – I just sat there modestly with a scarf over my hair like a good little girl, as is fitting in an Islamic country! As a reward, the man who was renting us the car told me that we would feel at home in his car because the driver could speak good English and wore a uniform. I immediately put on a happy expression, so that he could be certain that we had a uniformed chauffeur at home too. You have to keep up appearances! So tomorrow is the big day. It's really lovely to be back in the Orient.

As always, when a dream comes to fruition, one you have been viewing from a great distance for years, and are on the point of fulfilling – and in our case that means being at the starting point of our journey, now on the 1st of May 1998 in Islamabad – you can hardly believe that everything is real and that you are the same person. But it is true! We are really sitting in the lovely garden of the Ambassador Hotel and are feeling great.

4. From Islamabad to Gilgit on the Karakoram Highway

Today it's already Sunday May 3rd. We only arrived here in Pakistan two days ago, and I really don't know where to begin telling my story. At the moment I'm sitting in Gilgit on the terrace outside our room.

We set out from Islamabad at seven o'clock yesterday morning. I've already mentioned that we'd rented a car with a driver. That was on the afternoon of the 1st of May. That evening, as we were waiting for our dinner in the garden of the Ambassador Hotel, the brother of the owner of the car rental firm suddenly appeared, accompanied by a Mister Nissar, the manager, with whom we'd negotiated and signed the rental contract that afternoon. They sat down at the table with us and started to talk to one another excitedly. All we understood were place names like Gilgit, Chilas, Dasu and others. With some effort, we worked out that they obviously wished to persuade us to travel to Gilgit in a single day. Of course we did not want that, because we could have flown for a fraction of the price! And above all, we wanted to see a lot of things and make a lot of stops. When they saw that we were not going to be persuaded, the owner of the car rental company was sent for in person. Now he was also sitting at our table, in the middle of our dinner – we didn't let him spoil it –, knocking his knees nervously together the whole time, while his brother kept holding his mobile fervently to his ear, even though nobody called and he didn't call anybody either. They didn't actually tell us exactly what they wanted, but they kept behaving as if they only had our best interests at heart.

When they realised that we were not to be deterred, everything finally returned to square one. The only thing was that we were warned not to make excessive demands on the driver, and not to ask him to stop too often. The five-year-old son of the car rental man, who was there as well and had been staring wide-eyed at our meal, was made to shake everyone's hand, and finally they assured us that they had only come to ensure that everything was to our satisfaction.

At the word 'satisfaction' Horst suddenly thought of something very important: he asked if the hired car had air-conditioning. But in true Pakistani fashion the car-hire man, never at a loss for an answer, said that 'Air Condition' didn't start until the 15th of May.

At this very moment, all the muezzins in Gilgit are starting to call the faithful to prayer – and strangely enough, all the goats are starting to bleat at the very same moment!

Horst is just coming with our last little British Airways bottle of Bordeaux, and we'll drink it now overlooking the view of the Gilgit River.

After downing the wine it was too dark to write, because the electricity here is not very good. The lamps provide very little light and there are constant power cuts. [Only next morning was it possible to take up our text again.]

From Islamabad we set off – as I've already said – for Gilgit at 7:15 in the morning. Our driver's 'uniform' admittedly consisted only of dark blue trousers and a white shirt and his English was less than mediocre, but he made up for that by his calm and careful driving style, which we learned to value, especially when we reached the Karakoram Highway, the KKH.

It was only when we left Islamabad that we really got the feeling of being in Pakistan. Even if the airport itself is very Pakistani, Islamabad itself strikes you as extremely modern. But a few kilometres out of Islamabad things became very oriental: cows, goats, people, carts, cars, heavily laden, brightly painted, hooting lorries, dirt and stench, total confusion. As far as Taxila we were still on the Grand Trunk Road, and then the KKH began. At first there was still a terrible amount of traffic, but after Manshera, a long ribbon-developed village, the road became so empty that for quite a while we thought the driver had got lost – we felt sure this was so because he had hesitated at one junction as if uncertain which road to take. Since all the signposts and town signs were exclusively in Arabic script it took about an hour and a half for us to realise that we were actually on the right road.

The junction in Manshera led to an unmetalled track over the 4,173 metre high Babusar Pass through the mountains: Nanga Parbat is only 50 kilometres away. The track over the pass joins the KKH again at Chilas. Since from the middle of July to the end of September this stretch is only passable with a four-wheel-drive vehicle, our driver naturally chose the better road along the Indus Valley. In the past, before the KKH was built, the track over the Babusar Pass was an important trade route to the south.

After the junction the landscape became ever wilder and more mountainous, and even the people in the villages seemed more untamed and unapproachable. The people's faces became serious, impenetrable or even forbidding. The further we travelled along the KKH, the more women we saw who were totally veiled, ultimately more than half of them.

Ill. 6 and 7:
Top-heavy, overloaded lorries

Ill. 8: From Rawalpindi to Pishora

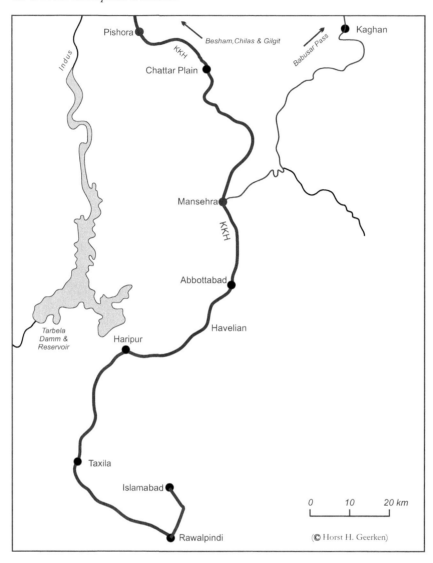

After Dasu, where we spent the night, we saw hardly any women in the streets. We arrived here in Gilgit yesterday afternoon, and between then and this afternoon we have only caught sight of five women.

From Thakot onwards the KKH winds along the right bank of the Indus, rising all the time. Gloomy grey-black, bare mountains tower on both sides of the river. The Indus rages down towards the Indian Ocean: in Besham its loud roar drowns out the sound of your own voice.

Ill. 9: On the KKH

Ill. 10: Crumbling bridges on our route

Ill. 11: From Pishora to Shatial

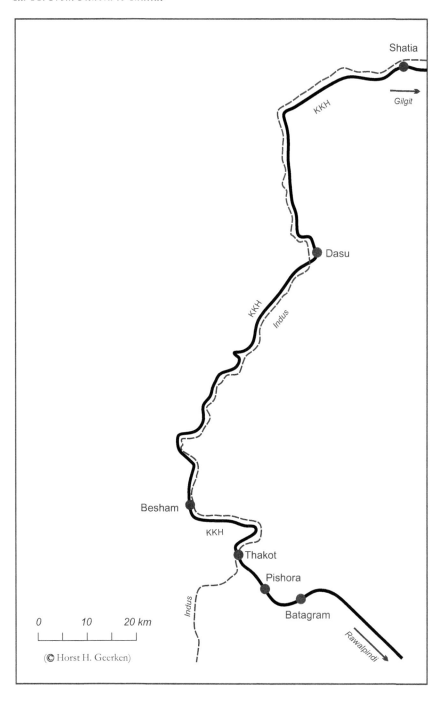

Hundreds of inscriptions and images carved in the cliffs and large rocks along the Indus are like a guest book of the Silk Road. In many languages, the vicissitudes of the relationship between China and the Indus valley are recorded here. In the past, exotic goods streamed out of the Indus Valley to the rest of the world.

Just beyond Besham is the famous milestone at the edge of the KKH: still 975 kilometres to Kashgar! We've covered a quarter of the distance.

Ill. 12: Still 975 kilometres from Kashgar!
Ill. 13: Suspension bridge over the Indus

But back to our journey from when the road reached the Indus. From that point on it really became unimaginably adventurous and dangerous. You have to have seen it! A wildly threatening mountain landscape, the road not stable, falling steeply away on one side – up to 150 metres deep – down to the river, and on the other side of the river equally steeply rising cliffs up to the snow covered peaks. Again and again we came to places where the road had been covered by a landslide and a new road had been created by simply shovelling a way over the landslide, which, of course, could slide further at

Ill. 14: Obstacles on the KKH
Ill. 15: Occasionally you had to guess where the road was.

any moment. Every time we had to drive over one of those bits, I sent up a hurried prayer. And rock falls everywhere – though the rocks that fall in those parts are more like minor cliffs. One of them, about the size of my living room, must have crashed down on the road just before we got there. Fortunately it had fallen at an angle that meant that we could just squeeze past in the car.

Again and again we had to cross both large and small streams which simply flowed over the road in great floods: every time we feared we'd be washed off into the depths below. Twice we even drove through waterfalls.

The rock falls made our driver particularly nervous. He literally hung over the steering wheel for the whole journey so that he could look up at the mountains above to see if anything was threatening to crash down on us. Presumably rock falls were the greatest danger on this journey. At any rate, it seemed miraculous to us that we weren't hit by anything.

We passed Abottabad, a town at an altitude of 1,200 metres, during the morning. The people in the relatively infrequent settlements were beginning by now to look as if they came from the Old Testament. In Dasu, which we reached in the late afternoon, we intended initially to stay in the government guesthouse, the CW-Guesthouse just above Dasu, which we had chosen from Horst's guidebook. The food was supposed to be excellent, cooked by a Kohistani chef. But the guesthouse seemed totally deserted, and the manager was down in the village – nobody knew exactly when he might return. So we decided to take a room down in Dasu village – which is, by the way, the district capital of Kohistan, so that a Kohistani chef is unlikely to be a rarity there – in the Arafat Hotel right on the bank of the Indus. The room had a splendid view over the river, was clean but musty – and there was electricity only in the evening. But I suppose if cars only have air-conditioning after the 15th of May, it's only fair that there should be no current in hotel rooms until the evening! The chef in the hotel was Kashmiri, which seemed more remarkable to me than a Kohistani. He cooked us an excellent meal, but afterwards we needed a double Fernet Branca and a Whisky because of the excessively fatty food. We'd already eaten a meal in a very indigenous guesthouse in the little village of Besham. Our systems are not used to such quantities of fat in dhal, vegetables and rice – they never make white rice, but only a kind of greasy pilaf. It all tasted good, but afterwards we felt as if we had a large lump of fat in our stomachs.

Ill. 16: Dasu is a dull grey city
Ill. 17: Dasu, Arafat Hotel

Horst had great difficulty getting to sleep that night in Dasu. Firstly, there was a lorry going crazy on the bridge over the Indus near the hotel. The driver was hooting continuously; then there was a great palaver in the restaurant beneath us when two people set about each other. When the outside world finally came to rest, I was snoring! I didn't hear any of the night's events. The last I heard was the rushing of the Indus und the thundering of the great rocks that kept on falling from the mountains into the valley below: apart from that, I slept extremely well the whole night. Horst, however, had wild dreams during the night of the 2nd to the 3rd of May.

It rained heavily throughout that night, as it had done on the previous day as we drove through the mountains. My first words the next morning were, "Anita had a healthy boy last night," and I told Annette about my dream: my niece Anita was pacing up and down in the room with a very swollen belly, carrying a glass in her hand, from which she kept on drinking. Finally she disappeared into her bedroom. Shortly afterwards she came back smiling with her little boy in her arms and showed him to me.

The dream was so realistic that I immediately sent a postcard to Anita, and on the 21st of May we received a birth announcement in Gulmit: Anita had given birth to her son that very night!

The next morning shortly after 8 o'clock we continued our journey. As far as Chilas the road was said to be in great danger of rock falls – and we saw them everywhere. Here in the Karakoram mountains the Eurasian and Asiatic plates collide, and that's why the earth is so unsettled in this area. It is a great experience to drive through this landscape on this precipitous road, but I felt uneasy the whole time – especially when we had to cross a landslide or a temporary bridge where the original had been ripped away, or squeeze past giant blocks of stone on the road.

Chilas used to be a dangerous den of robbers, but now it's a popular trading centre at the crossing of several routes. This is where the track over the Babusar Pass rejoins the KKH. Beyond Chilas the valley widened and we felt more relaxed – especially our driver. The landscape is desolate and inhospitable: it was only where there were settlements that we saw lush patches of green. They are oases irrigated by water brought to the villages from the glaciers by channels. And you only find human dwellings where irrigation is possible.

Shortly after leaving Chilas the Nanga Parbat Massif suddenly hove into view in all its grandeur and majesty, gleaming in the morning sun. The weather had brightened and the sun had finally shown itself. What a gigantic view – we couldn't take our eyes off the mountain. The previous days we had been subjected to a continuous downpour, which did nothing to make the journey less scary.

We came to a junction with a signpost: "Fairy Meadows". We had to see this famous sight, and asked our driver to drive up the gravel track – which he did, albeit somewhat reluctantly. The Fairy Meadows lie high up in the Rakhiot Valley at an altitude of about 3,500 metres. When you arrive there from the desert-like Indus Valley, the blooming alpine meadows are quite a surprise. This is where the many German Nanga Parbat expeditions started out. The base camp was only a little higher up, but could only be reached on foot.

Nanga Parbat – the Naked Mountain – is, at an altitude of 8,125 metres, one of the ten highest mountains in the world. The mountain face to the south – 4,500 metres high – is the steepest and highest in the world. Alpinists consider Nanga Parbat to be the most difficult mountain to climb, and many mountaineers and native porters have lost their lives there. Temperatures are often far below zero and constant gusts of wind at speeds of some 100 kilometres per hour make the climb almost impossible. The freezing temperatures are the least of their problems.

Mountaineering became fashionable in Britain towards the end of the 19th century and the first Alpine Club in the world was founded in London. In 1885 a Briton, Alfred Mummery, was the first mountaineer to attempt to conquer Nanga Parbat. In August he set out with two bearers. All three were buried by a huge avalanche. They were never found.

From July 1932 there were several attempts to be the first to climb the mountain by German alpinists. They all ended in tragedy. The experienced German mountaineer and expedition leader Willy Merkel lost his life in a snowstorm. In 1934 four German climbers and six native Sherpas died on the mountain. The greatest height reached was just over 7,000 metres.

After the foundation of the German Himalaya Foundation in 1936, the third Nanga Parbat expedition under the Third Reich, a team of experienced mountaineers led by Karl Wien, set off in 1937. A memorial tablet for the dead of the Merkel expedition was set up at the foot of Nanga Parbat. The Wien expedition also ended in disaster: seven German climbers and nine Sherpas were buried by an avalanche. The surviving Sherpas fled down to the valley: they were certain that the mountain goddess Peri had struck again. Karl Wien and most of

Ill. 18: Nanga Parbat[13]

Ill. 19: The Fairy Meadows[14]

13 https://commons.wikimedia.org/wiki/File%3ANanga_parbat_abdul_rafey.jpg
14 Copyrighted for free use by https://en.wikipedia.org/wiki/Fairy_Meadows#/media/File:Nanga_parbat,_fairy_medow,_Pak_by_gul791.jpg

the members of the expedition were dead, and only the two scientists who had remained in the camp, Uli Luft and the Bonn Professor Karl Troll, survived.

Paul Friedrich Peter Bauer, a climber from Munich, was a major in the Mountain Infantry and the leading personality in National Socialist mountain sports. He had previous experience in the Himalayas in expeditions in 1929 and 1931 to Kanchenjunga, at 8,586 metres the third highest mountain in the world.

When the news of the failure of the Nanga Parbat expedition reached Germany, Bauer organised a search and rescue operation, aided by two other experienced climbers. However, because of the start of winter this could only be launched the following summer.

A Junkers Ju 52 was put at their disposal by the German Luftwaffe. It was their intention to get as close as possible to the site of the disaster. The pilot was Lex Thoenes, also a mountaineer with Himalayan experience. The aircraft had to make an emergency landing near Lahore because of damage to the steering gear. Bauer's group set out from here for Nanga Parbat on foot, accompanied for their protection by a number of British-Indian soldiers. After the Ju 52 was repaired it flew on to Srinagar in Kashmir, from where Lex Thoenes made a supply flight to the main camp on Nanga Parbat. The supplies were dropped and it was possible to collect them. It was the first time that an aircraft had been used for support on Nanga Parbat.

Bauer made three recovery attempts. He found the victims of the disaster entombed in the ice several metres beneath the snow. He also succeeded in recovering some bodies from the camp of the Merkel Expedition. However, he did not reach the peak of Nanga Parbat.

A new expedition with Heinrich Harrer and Peter Aufschnaiter was interrupted by the Second World War. Since they were at the time on the territory of what was then British India, they were interned in the Dehra Dun camp in North India. I have described this – and their escape – in my book "Hitler's Asian Adventure".[15]

It was not until 1953 that Hermann Buhl made the first successful ascent in a 41-hour solo climb. Karl Maria Herrligkoffer, a Munich doctor and half-brother of Willy Merkel, led eight further expeditions to Nanga Parbat between 1953 and 1975, in which several more lives were lost. In 1970 the Messner brothers made a second successful ascent, though on the descent Günther Messner was killed. In 1978 his brother Reinhold climbed the mountain again, this time solo. In 2013 11 climbers were shot in the base camp by Taliban terrorists.

---

15 p. 168f

Given so many disasters it is hardly any wonder that Nanga Parbat, the only 8,000-metre peak in the western Himalayas, has gone down in history as the 'Bane of the Germans' and 'Killer Mountain'.

When my brother Hartmut visited the Hunza Valley in May 1974, he found a large number of packets of German egg pasta labelled NANGA PARBAT EXPEDITION HERRLIGKOFFER in a little kiosk in Karimabad. Herrligkoffer visited Nanga Parbat several times between 1964 and 1972. Presumably the pasta was left over from the 1972 expedition, and it was a welcome addition to my brother's diet and still tasted excellent to him.

Today there are wooden huts and tents for rent on the Fairy Meadows. Since the season was just beginning, we were the first foreigners there that year. We would have liked to stay longer at this historic site, but our driver was insistent: he wanted to reach Gilgit by daylight. We spent a minute's silence in memory of the many climbers and Pakistani porters who had died there.

We enjoyed the infinite silence and unbounded beauty of the place, although it was now raining gently again and the sky was once more cloudy. Then we carried on. Again and again we saw Buddhist images and ancient rock drawings which Buddhist pilgrims and merchants had left on the Silk Road. I had previously seen similar rock drawings in Ladakh in western Tibet, although none of the Silk Roads passed through there.

For twenty years about 10,000 Chinese and 15,000 Pakistani workers laboured under extreme climatic conditions to hack the most difficult road in the world out of the almost vertical cliff walls. In the Indus Valley in summer the heat is extreme and in the pass regions there is equally extreme cold. Almost 1,000 human lives were lost during the construction until the entire KKH could finally be opened to traffic in 1986. Some stretches of the KKH were opened in 1982 and from then on locals could travel on it without special permits. It is a two-lane, roughly 1,300 kilometre highway through an inhospitable landscape which joins western China with Pakistan via the Hunza Valley between the Karakoram, Hindu Kush, Pamir and Himalaya ranges. It can only be travelled in summer. Its highest point is the Khunjerab Pass, the border between Pakistan and China, at an altitude of 5,000 metres. The Khunjerab Pass is the highest paved international pass in the world, and the KKH the highest trunk road. The KKH is not just a gigantic engineering feat – maintaining it will also be a great challenge.

Ill. 20: The KKH to Gilgit

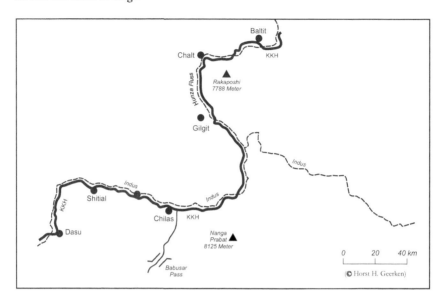

What is the purpose of this road, that has cost so many lives and so much tribulation? Trade along the highway is so far minimal. From Pakistan to China they export cigarettes, the brightly coloured fabrics that are so popular in Kashgar, dried fruit, medical products and so on; from China to Pakistan tools, bicycles, electrical goods, tea and coal. Because it is regularly blocked by landslides, floods and rock falls, the road is of minor military and strategic importance. It is meant more as a symbol of Sino-Pakistani friendship in response to Indo-Russian rapprochement. Nevertheless, the road still facilitates Beijing's long-held wish for a transit route from China to the Indian subcontinent and the Indian Ocean. It intensifies the active and friendly relationship between Pakistan and China. But, as I said, it is often blocked for days at a time: this is where the continental plates collide, the Indian plate pushing under the Eurasian plate. These massive forces cause the mountains to grow by five to ten millimetres a year, more than is washed away by erosion.

At the same time, nature appears to be defending itself against the attacks by the powerful road-building explosions. Every day massive blocks of stone tumble down onto the road; landslides sweep whole sections of road down into the depths. The local inhabitants say that the steep mountainsides have been made unstable by the explosions. Initially the Hunzakuts rebelled against the introduction of the Chinese building workers. They were protesting at the intrusion of foreign forces into their mountain world.

Everywhere and all the time someone is at work, by hand with shovels, but also with large machines. Landslides and rock falls are cleared away, new road beds bulldozed out of the detritus. The KKH is a road through extremely high mountains which are home to a river culture with hanging gardens and hanging roads on the steep mountain slopes. It often looks as if little green patches have been cut out of some lush, fertile land and then stuck on the crags of this bare mountain wilderness. How do they get up there? Apparently the people of the region learn to climb before they learn to walk.

Round every bend new, breathtaking snowy peaks appear. High up on the crags run the channels cut out of the rock to carry the water from the glaciers to the villages and fields – often a distance of up to 80 kilometres. You can only distinguish the channels because of the narrow strips of wild green vegetation made possible by the glacier water.

The KKH will never be finished. I often had the feeling that humankind can do nothing against the primal force of the mountains, and that in twenty or thirty years the road will no longer exist. A single big landslide is enough to block the most exciting highway in the world for days or weeks. Nature is always stronger – it will win!

Just beyond Jaglot the Indus turns to the east towards Skardu, and so we now left the Indus and followed the River Hunza upwards. Shortly afterwards we passed an impressive monument. This is where the Karakoram, Hindu Kush and Himalaya ranges meet and in the near vicinity there are three of the highest mountains in the world, K2, at 8,611 metres the highest mountain in the Karakoram and second highest in the world, Nanga Parbat, at 8,125 metres the only 8,000 metre peak in the western Himalayas, and Tirich Mir, at 7,708 metres the highest mountain in the Hindu Kush.

On top of the monument there is a viewing terrace with a magnificent view of the snow-covered peaks of this mountainous world. Unfortunately, there had been no improvement in the weather, and the clouds were very low. Written on the monument in large letters is:

'THE JUNCTION POINT OF THREE GREATEST MOUNTAIN RANGES OF THE WORLD'

And there is a tablet with the following inscription:

'THE KARAKORAM, THE HINDUKUSH AND THE HIMALAYAN RANGES MEET HERE AT THE CONFLUENCE OF THE INDUS AND GILGIT RIVERS. EAST ACROSS THE INDUS IS THE HIMA-

LAYA, KARAKORAM IN THE NORTH AND IN THE WEST THE HINDUKUSH.
THE HIMALAYA IS ABOUT 2,400 KM LONG, RUNS THROUGH INDIA, PAKISTAN, CHINA, BHUTAN AND NEPAL. THE KARAKORAM, 500 KM LONG, LIES MOSTLY IN GILGIT-BALTISTAN OF PAKISTAN. THE 966 KM LONG HINDUKUSH RANGE STRADDLES BOTH PAKISTAN AND AFGHANISTAN.'

In 2010 there was a major landslide near Attabad, which blocked the River Hunza, creating the 27-kilometre long Lake Attabad, which now has to be crossed using simple ferries. Since there are doubts about the stability of the dam created by the landslide, about 15,000 people in 36 villages down-river are in great danger.

In the afternoon, just after 4 p.m., we arrived in Gilgit, excited by our journey over the first part of the KKH, but also glad that we would not have to make this dangerous journey again when we return: we are going to fly back. Our driver, after dropping us off and pocketing his tip, set off immediately on his return journey to Rawalpindi and Islamabad.

This is the beginning of the Pamir Knot, which in the century before last was the focus of the power struggle between Britain and Russia – and also China.

In Gilgit we stayed in the Hunza Inn, simple and as clean as could be expected in Pakistan. The pride of the hotel is its carpet, but it has never seen a vacuum cleaner! We had to have the bathroom cleaned, but then we felt quite comfortable. The proprietor, Abdullah Baig, is very helpful, and ever since he heard that we don't eat meat we can hardly stop him making chips for us! He obviously regards them as the *non plus ultra* in the life of a vegetarian! We only avoided this yesterday because we came across a hotel called the Ibex as we wandered through the bazaar. We went in, because we had looked at all possible smaller hotels during our pre-trip researches. It was gloomy, down-at-heel, dirty – and then suddenly light at the end of a dark corridor: the restaurant! The staff were extremely friendly: the hotel was being refurbished at the time, so it wasn't possible to stay there, but we could eat there, said the staff. The restaurant was bright and friendly, though the tablecloths were quite dirty – they should perhaps have been included in the refurbishment, but I suppose you shouldn't be too picky. There were a whole lot of locals there. The tea they served us was hot and tasted good, and so we ate a spinach dish with chapatti, which was excellent and certainly

Ill. 21: For an engineer a bridge like this one over the Indus is always something special

Ill. 22: The highest mountain ranges in the world meet here

Ill. 23: Street in Gilgit
Ill. 24: Fruit and vegetable sellers

did not kill us. On the way home we bought some fruit and here in the hotel we were given yoghourt as well – so yesterday we escaped the chips, but this evening we've ordered dinner here – let's see if there are the inevitable chips, or whether Horst has managed to persuade the proprietor just to serve us vegetables and rice.

At lunchtime today we bought cucumber, onions, garlic, yoghourt and hot, fresh flatbread in the bazaar, and to the surprise of the natives made a cucumber salad with flatbread here in the hotel. It tasted really good. After only a few days here you begin to need something fresh and not so fatty. So we can now look forward to our evening meal with equanimity.

Unlike other markets in Pakistan we didn't have to haggle here. We always got the same price as the locals, and we were always given hot tea and cakes, even if we didn't buy anything. You could find almost anything here, from jewels through dried fruit, crockery and flowers to Chinese silk. The variety on offer was staggering. As a result of the KKH, trade with China had been revived at Gilgit, that once important trading post on the Silk Road.

We originally intended not to travel into the Hunza Valley until today, the 6th of May, but we have actually been here since yesterday evening and can only now record our experiences in Gilgit. Everything was different from what we had planned. Yesterday morning we went for a drive around Gilgit with our host, Abdullah Baig. It was beautiful, truly idyllic and rural. We saw the Kagah-Buddha carved high up in the rock and walked along beside one of the channels that take the water from the glaciers to the oases. The Kagah or Gilgit Buddha is about three metres tall, and all around it there are holes carved in the rock face at regular intervals, and the rock is also carved out between the holes. There are two explanations for the carvings and the holes according to Abdullah Baig: either there was originally a wooden shrine around the Buddha, or the British had made an attempt to take the Buddha out of the rock to put it in one of their museums.

On the trip we also passed the British cemetery. We wanted to visit it, but our Abdullah Baig dismissed it curtly with the words, "You don't have to see that, the British people have been very cruel to us". The relationship with the British seems to be as dysfunctional as ever!

At the end of our trip we got them to drop us off at the Post Office so that we could post some letters and postcards. The Post Office seemed to me to be totally disorganised – which it was –, but when we looked more closely we found a man who had stamps laid out in front of him. That got us a

Ill. 25 and 26: At the market

bit further, but after we'd stuck stamps on all our post, getting our fingers sticky in the process, we couldn't find anyone to take our correspondence and stamp it. We finally understood what people had been trying to explain to us with hand and foot gestures: we had to leave the Post Office and go out round the back. There was a kind of stable door in the rear which we had to pass through, ending up in a very dark space. When our eyes became used to the darkness, we saw a man at the end of the room, who was rummaging around in an unimaginable pile of letters and did actually take our post and even stamp it. Will it ever reach its destination?[16] We would also have liked to send a fax, but then we learned that they definitely never reach their intended recipients.

When we arrived back in the Hotel Hunza Inn after this business, Abdullah Baig was waiting for us devotedly, only to tell us that we would have to leave for Karimabad that very day because religious disturbances were expected the next day. We already knew that an important Islamic festival about which the Sunnis and Shiites had very different views was in the offing, but we had been told that things would only get uncomfortable the next day, when we had intended to leave for Karimabad anyway. In Gilgit there are frequent religious festivals like this, leading to bloody clashes between Sunnis and Shiites, and then as a tourist you cannot leave your hotel or travel on the Karakoram Highway. You are forced to wait until tempers have cooled once more.

The day before we had already asked our host – and new friend – Abdullah Baig, who had obviously taken us into his heart so much that he was really concerned about our welfare and constantly trying to help us in every possible way, for advice about a transaction that we wished to make on behalf of a friend of the Rosinys. We were supposed to take the money required to pay for the schooling of a young boy to a village called Hussainabad.

Rosiny's acquaintance had been on a trekking tour in the Hunza Valley with some friends, and the father of the boy he had sponsored ever since that time had been the expedition's cook. It was all a bit complicated, because there was also a teacher who was felt to be rather shady, and whom the donor of the money thought likely to pocket the money for himself if it got into his hands. So we asked Abdullah Baig about Hussainabad and how we should best proceed.

And as chance would have it, Abdullah Baig was originally from Hussainabad. He knew the cook and the teacher, whom he also felt to be un-

---

16 It did arrive – the most unexpected things do happen!

Ill. 27: Above the Indus Valley with Abdullah Baig
Ill. 28: Along the channel

trustworthy. So he decided at once to take us to Hussainabad and to help us to deal with the matter. Since we were now having to leave a day earlier, we were at first worried that Abdullah Baig might not be able to come with us, but he regarded it as a matter of course. He is anyway more concerned with the finer things in life than with commercial profit, as can easily be seen from the way he runs his hotel! Sitting in the garden chatting with friends – or, if he likes them, hotel guests – is more important to him than keeping the hotel in order. He is also a member of the geological society and gave us a lot of interesting geological information.

5. Into the Hunza Valley from Gilgit to Karimabad

We set off at 2 p.m. Our freshly washed clothes – still damp – were put in plastic bags. We were in a hurry to get away, but there was no escape from the threatened chips from Abdullah Baig's kitchen. He sent a boy with a plateful of fatty chips, a dish of dhal[17] and a flatbread to us: on the house! We had actually intended to have the dhal the evening before, but the cook had forgotten it, and we'd ordered the flatbread for breakfast, but that had been forgotten, too. To the delight of the noble donor, we ate all the chips, thus confirming him in the belief that, for a vegetarian, nothing is as much like heaven on earth as chips. But he is really a very witty and smart guy, even if his hotel is sinking into chaos and is not to be recommended to the more sensitive traveller. But after the flatbread, chips and dhal, nothing more stood in the way of our departure.

Once again, the journey was breathtaking. First of all, close to Gilgit we came to the place where the two torrential rivers, the Gilgit and the Hunza, join. It is a foaming water-inferno with a thousand eddies. A swimmer would have no chance here. Even the entrance to the Hunza Valley was a great experience.

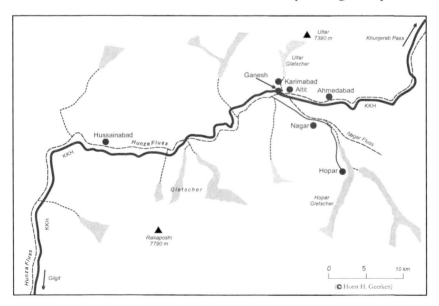

Ill. 29: From Gilgit to Karimabad

---

17 A spicy lentil dish

As late as the end of the 19th century the valley could only be reached by a narrow, dangerous path over a 4,000-metre-high pass and rickety, makeshift rope bridges. Now we arrived at a narrow, wooden suspension bridge over a deep ravine, leading directly to a dark hole in the opposite, almost vertical cliff. This narrow bridge, swaying in the wind, didn't exactly inspire confidence. That was going to bear the weight of our Suzuki minibus? Annette wanted to get out, but Abdullah Baig reassured her. He had crossed this bridge many times before.

Once we were on the bridge, it didn't look half as dilapidated, but it swung alarmingly back and forth in the wind. The clattering planks of the bridge even looked relatively new. The minibus inched its way slowly along the narrow roadway until we reached the dark hole. Once we got there, we had solid ground under our wheels again.

The roadway that was chiselled out of the mountain like a rocky cave, a narrow, dark track, wound steeply upwards in broad spirals. The aperture in the mountain was so small that there were only a few inches between the sides and the roof of the minibus. Annette closed her eyes. This adventure was a bit too much for her. When we finally emerged into daylight, we were in the Hunza Valley which, starting as a narrow gap, opened wide in front of us.

Hunza is a completely different world, with a wild landscape! We met friendly, open people – a blessing after the dark looks of the Kohistanis, who have no time for foreigners.

In the Indus Valley we'd already seen and admired the rock drawings, but here, as soon as we reached the Hunza Valley, the ground was strewn with large rocks engraved with prehistoric drawings of human figures, hunting scenes, animals, sun discs, demons and gods. Drawings of stags were particularly frequent, even though there are no stags in the Indus and Hunza Valleys. From the time of the earliest human wanderings in this region onwards, the rock drawings have been a medium of cultural communication and provide evidence of amazing cultural diversity. The extremely dry climate has helped to preserve the art works for many centuries. Forgotten languages and literatures were discovered. The use of line in the animal drawings was surprisingly elegant. We also saw horses with and without riders, a Buddha on a lotus flower and sun symbols. According to Abdullah Baig some figures go back to the 3rd millennium B.C. Many of the images and scripts have still not been interpreted or deciphered.

Since the end of the 1970s German ethnologists have worked on deciphering these petroglyphs. Their researches have provided a new source for interpreting lo-

Ill. 30 and 31: The entrance to the Hunza Valley

Ill. 32: A dour, dry welcome from the lower Hunza Valley

Ill. 33.1: Rock drawings near Gilgit

Ill. 33.2 and 33.3: Rock drawings near Gilgit[18]

---

18 At the end of this book there are other photographs of rock drawings in black and white, taken by Hans Bräker during his trip in 1976 (Ill. 132-135)

cal history and have made an important contribution to research into the Asiatic trade routes known as the Silk Roads.[19]

Our driver, a young 17-year-old man from Karimabad, kept looking up at the mountains above to see if there were any rocks about to descend on us. I was a bit afraid that he might – as he had done on that morning's trip around Gilgit – switch off the engine on downhill stretches to save petrol, but fortunately he did not do that on this hair-raising road. He was an excellent driver in spite of his age and the fact that he didn't have a driving licence yet. That was why Abdullah Baig became nervous every time we saw a policeman, because if we had been checked, he would have been fined.

On the other side of the river it was frequently possible to see the remains of the old road, which is actually little more than a narrow path adhering to the almost vertical cliff faces: all that is left of the old Silk Road. Again and again I saw gangs of workers who were improving the old caravan path and trying to make it passable on foot again. From a distance this narrow path can only be seen as a light incision in the precipitous rock face. That path would certainly be no good for us, because Annette has no head for heights.

Many small settlements can be seen hanging high up on small plateaus in the rock face. Every available square yard is devoted to the cultivation of maize or corn. Along the edges of these fields they grow bright flowers, which serve to warn the farmers that this is the edge of the abyss. There is nothing but a narrow, break-neck path carved into the rock to connect the settlement to the valley. Everything here is mountaineering. The Hunzakuts must be able to climb like mountain goats!

All of a sudden all the traffic came to a halt: a landslide! But the army was already in action and was clearing the roadway with a powerful bulldozer. We hadn't expected a problem so soon. A Swiss man, who had come from Karimabad and moved into our hotel in Gilgit that lunch time, had told us about a gigantic landslide about an hour from Gilgit which he had had to climb over with some difficulty and which would definitely take at least three days to clear. He clearly didn't know the Pakistani Army! When we

---

19 This project – like the expeditions of 1955, 1964, 1973 and 1975 – was financially supported by the Deutsche Forschungsgemeinschaft [German Research Association] DFG. The results are clear to see: A good 1,500 inscriptions and 10,000 rock drawings were discovered. [Karl Jettmar, *Zwischen Gandhara und den Seidenstraßen, Entdeckungen deutsch-pakistanischer Expeditionen {Between Gandhara and the Silk Roads: Discoveries by German-Pakistani expeditions 1979 – 1984}*, Mainz, p. 10] In 1984 this long-term project was handed over to the Heidelberger Akademie der Wissenschaften [Heidelberg Academy of Sciences].

arrived only hours later the road had been roughly cleared, and although it was difficult we still got through in our minibus.

Great masses of detritus are regularly detached from the steep mountainsides by ice, sun and rain. They block the KKH, making it impassable for days or even weeks. Hundreds of road-workers and vehicles have been buried along the course of the KKH.

Towards four o'clock we came to the turning for Hussainabad. That was the right road for me! I always had to sit in the front, because the men were in the back, and of course in Islamic Pakistan it was not proper for a woman to sit among the men: morality must be preserved! But this meant that I could see everything that approached us. We had to cross an extremely threatening looking suspension bridge which was approached by a steep beaten path of earth and stones: I was afraid we'd slide on it even before reaching the bridge. Horst and Abdullah Baig had to "calm" the bridge itself down because the wind was blowing it up so strongly that the bus couldn't cross the threshold. It took quite a while to press the swaying bridge far enough down for the wheels of our vehicle to gain traction on the planks of the bridge.

After we'd crossed that unsteady construction high over the foaming Hunza River, we had to drive along the old Hunza road which is not metalled at all, but simply cut out of the slope or made passable by layers of stones. To our right a steep cliff fell almost vertically down to the raging river, and to our left it towered upwards just as steeply. So I'm sure no one will be surprised that I was totally indifferent to the beauties of the landscape and just closed my eyes. I just didn't want to see where we would fall if the road crumbled away beneath us. And it seemed to me inevitable that the road, which was exactly the width of our bus, would slip away. On some of the very narrow bends one of the front wheels frequently hung out over the abyss. It was an uncanny and unpleasant feeling. Nobody spoke. All you could hear was the thundering Hunza River, which drowned out all other sounds.

When we arrived in Hussainabad we were lucky enough to find the man for whom the money was intended immediately with Abdullah Baig's help. He was sitting having tea with some friends on the steps of the community hall. A little palaver on both sides and our mission was fulfilled. Whether all of this was any use was something we weren't too sure about. It was really a most peculiar encounter. The man the money was meant for, the trekking cook, Shrukrullah Baig, was very reticent, as if he were afraid that we were checking up on him. He didn't invite us into his home, which was most unusual, in fact he didn't even offer us a cup of tea.

Ill. 34: A landslide is cleared

Ill. 35: A bridge to Hussainabad

He was supposed to be using the money for his son's education, but in spite of being asked several times, he did not call for his son to be fetched to meet his patron's friends, which was also very strange. Then we got him at least to show us the school his son was going to, and we realised that he wasn't sending him to the very good Aga Khan School that his patrons in Germany were paying for, but to the much worse – and much cheaper – village school. We did not get the impression that the money was being used for the boy in the way that the Rosinys' friend intended.

After spending a little more time in the village – Abdullah Baig introduced us to his sister –, we carried on towards Karimabad. Abdullah Baig initially intended to take us about 20 km along the old Hunza road to the next village and there rejoin the KKH over yet another suspension bridge, but since a section of the Hunza road had fallen away, it was – to my delight and Horst's disappointment – not possible. The KKH was adventurous enough for me!

Our driver and Abdullah Baig told us that the KKH was particularly dangerous when it was raining. That was why the driver had been so nervous on the road from Islamabad to Gilgit: it had rained quite heavily for some of the time. Nevertheless, we arrived safe and sound in Karimabad. During the journey we had wondered why the old Hunza road only ran along the right bank of the river even though the left bank occasionally seemed more suitable. We finally realised that the left side of the river is Nagar territory, and the Hunzakuts and the Nagar people are linked by a historical feud in which there were very few peaceful interludes, as in the time when they both united to fight the British.

Our journey passed ribbons of glacier and moraines. Around each bend new white seven-thousand metre peaks came into view. There is no valley anywhere else in the world which is surrounded by so many seven-thousand metre peaks. The valley is sometimes so narrow that there is no room to travel beside the river: in those places the KKH has been blasted out of the overhanging rocks.

Karimabad: here we are on the "roof of the world", in the middle of the Hunza Valley! We've found a very nice, new and very clean hotel, whose name – World Roof Hotel – I simply can't fix in my mind. Every time anyone here asks where we are staying I stutter out another – always wrong – name such as Top Roof Hotel, World Top Hotel or World Hill Hotel. One very great advantage of our hotel is that it has warm, very warm blankets, because it's still very cold here and under the blankets it's as warm as toast. The other hotels we looked at all had just synthetic wool blankets, I still

Ill. 36: Our Mission in Hussainabad, from the left: the teacher and Shrukrullah Baig

Ill. 37: Where the Indian and Eurasian plates meet

remember all too well how we froze under them in Uzbekistan, and at the time it was much warmer in Uzbekistan!

On the World Roof Hotel's roof terrace we could really feel we were on the roof of the world. The weather finally improved. In the daytime we often sat here in the sun and enjoyed the magnificent view over the Hunza Valley, the Baltit Fort and the snow-covered peaks towering all around.

Karimabad is situated on a mountainside, and the whole place is laid out in terraces. Karimabad was named after the spiritual head of the Ismailites, Karim Aga Khan. In the past, it was, with its roughly 5,000 inhabitants, an important station for the caravans on the Silk Road from China to Kashmir and the Indian Ocean. It was known for its flourishing slave market.

Today the Aga Khan Foundation is very active. It runs schools, hospitals and workshops where young people are trained, the education of girls and young women being a particularly important focus. The illiteracy rate in the Hunza Valley is considerably lower than that in the rest of Pakistan. We were told that all Hunzakuts under 30 could read and write.

Prince Karim Aga Khan IV[20] *is the spiritual head of the Ismailites, a branch of Islam with 20 million adherents worldwide. Their religion is moderate and characterised by shamanistic influences. They are avowedly tolerant and open-minded.*

Prince Karim Aga Khan IV's father was the famous playboy Aly Khan, who married Hollywood star Rita Hayworth. Prince Karim became the head of the Ismailites after the death of his grandfather Aga Khan III in 1957.

His wealth is estimated at 10 billion Euros, making him one of the ten richest royals in the world. His Aga Khan Foundation is the biggest organisation for privately funded development projects. He is a major shareholder in many international concerns such as Lufthansa and earns around a billion Euros a year from his businesses. He also receives donations of several 100 million Euros per year from his adherents.

In 1998 he was married to the German Princess Gabriele zu Leiningen. She converted to Islam, receiving the title Begum Inaara Aga Khan. The couple separated in 2004, though they only finally divorced in 2011. The Princess had to renounce her title of Begum Inaara, but received alimony of 60 million Euros – she is unlikely to go hungry at any time during her life.

Prince Karim Aga Khan IV's Foundation supports a large number of private development projects in the fields of education, health, architecture, water supplies, and security of food supplies. All around the world he has founded Aga

---

20 His official name is Karim al-Husseini

Ill. 38: The World Roof Hotel

Ill. 39: On the hotel's roof terrace

Ill. 40: Karimabad and the Baltit Fort

Ill. 41: The Baltit Fort

Khan universities, schools, hospitals and training centres for craftsmen and teachers. Everywhere you go in the Hunza Valley you come across these Aga Khan development projects. In 1993 he founded the first high school in Karimabad exclusively for girls, with a boarding section.

Prince Aly Khan's father, that is, the grandfather of Karim Aga Khan IV, was Prince Sultan Mohammed Aga Khan III, who was President of the All India Muslim League and honoured as the 49th descendant of the Prophet Mohammed. He was a welcome guest at the British court. In 1937 this powerful Muslim leader was received by Adolf Hitler in Berchtesgaden and Joseph Goebbels in Berlin. Aga Khan showed great interest in the achievements and progress of the Third Reich. Hitler and Aga Khan were very impressed by each other. Hitler also mentioned in regard to Aga Khan, "England should allow us a free hand on the continent and we will not interfere in its overseas affairs."[21]

As documents that first came to light in 2008 reveal, Aga Khan III is supposed to have offered Adolf Hitler the support of a Muslim army in July 1942 – during the Second World War. Within a mere 10 to 15 days he would place 30,000 armed men at Hitler's disposal. Great Britain is said to have threatened him with the death penalty as a result of this.[22]

In Karimabad narrow, steep streets wind between the low wooden houses and the orderly orchards. Bright flowers – roses, lilies and zinnias – bloom everywhere. The terraced fields, where wheat, barley, beans, lentils, maize and all kinds of vegetables are cultivated, are mostly bordered by apricot trees, though there are sometimes poplars or birch trees. The potato was only introduced into the Hunza Valley at the beginning of the 20th century, and maize even later. In some fields seedtime was already over by the time we arrived.

The Mir decides on the time for seeding, which is celebrated by the festival of Bopao when the last snow has melted, between the beginning and middle of February. From time immemorial it has been seen as a combat between good and evil, light and darkness. The eternal sun that always triumphs over the darkness. The Bopao festival also signals the start of the polo season. In the higher regions of the Hunza Valley, in Gulmit or Passu, spring arrives later, so that Bopao is celebrated correspondingly later.

After the first furrow has been ploughed on the Mir's fields, he is given a dish of seeds, which he then mixes with gold dust. He then strews the seed in the furrow and wishes that Nature may provide strong and healthy crops. The Bopao festival

---

21 Paul Schmidt, *Statist auf diplomatischer Bühne* [partly translated as: *Hitler's Interpreter: The Secret History of German Diplomacy 1935-45*], pp. 343 and 375
22 *Hindustan Times*, 9th March 2008

took place a few weeks before we arrived and the seeds were already sprouting, so that the fields gleamed bright green with the young growth. Bopao is a spring festival with dancing and a feast provided from the Mir's granary. The ceremony represents the history of the creation of corn and bread.

The gold dust is washed from the Hunza River. In summer, when the early morning sun has not yet thawed the glaciers, water levels are quite low and the river less torrential. People then sail out on the river in their goatskin boats and fill them with river sand. Near the bank, the gold is washed out of the sand. Each of the gold-washers has to pay the king 15 grams of his booty in tribute.

The 700-year-old Baltit Fort, the former royal residence, dominates Karimabad. It was built in the Tibetan style, and reminded me of buildings I had previously seen in Ladakh in western Tibet. It was built on the summit of what the Hunzakuts call the cosmic mountain. This cultic kingdom regards the pillar in the middle of the palace as the centre of the world.

The Fort seemed quite run down and dilapidated to us, but the Hunzakuts assured us that a thorough renovation would begin the next year with the help of the Aga Khan Foundation. We groped our way via staircases and narrow corridors through various rooms in the semi-darkness and were glad to return to the daylight.

From the terrace above the polo field we had a remarkable view of Baltit, Altit and Ganesh. Behind us glaciers wound down to our level – the Hispar, Biafo, Baltoro and Siachen glaciers, the most massive glaciers outside the Antarctic. Looking up the valley we could follow the KKH for many kilometres into China. Rakaposhi with its cap of snow towered above the other peaks. It was a majestic view. We really had arrived on the Roof of the World!

For 70 years British climbers tried to conquer Rakaposhi. In 1958 an avalanche swept six Hunza bearers 1,500 metres into the depths below. Miraculously they all survived the fall. During this expedition two British climbers finally reached the summit.

Below the former palace, Mir Mohammad Nazim Tham built a new residence at the beginning of the last century, also in Tibetan style. Mir Gazanfar Ali still lives in this residence, having ascended to the – now only symbolic – throne on the death of his father in 1976.

We felt that we had been here before. Many things seemed familiar to us: strangely, the Hunza Valley did not seem at all alien to us. Here among these friendly people, we simply felt at home. Did this feeling derive from our many conversations with Annette's father and my brother, and the stories they had told us?

Ill. 42: View down into the Hunza Valley

Ill. 43: Karimabad, terraced building style

The Altit Fort lower down was just as ruinous as the Baltit Fort. When I visited the fort, I had the feeling it might collapse at any moment. It is about 200 years older than the Baltit Fort and is said to be the oldest building in the Hunza Valley.[23] The renovation of the fort in 2009 was funded by the Aga Khan Foundation.

A complicated irrigation system guarantees growth in the little fields that have been laid out on every available more or less level surface. From a distance the fields which have been created in terraces jutting out from the steep rock faces look like green patchwork. Centuries ago the Hunzakuts carved channels in the rock at audacious heights, and the channels still irrigate the fields using glacier water. It was and still is a bold project, since the channels are in need of constant maintenance and improvement.

No words are adequate to describe Hunza. The Asian explorer Eric Shipton wrote in 'Mountain of Tartary' in 1953, "It is difficult to describe the fantastic kingdom without indulging in superlatives." Two basic types of landscape which are only found separately in all other parts of the world merge into a single picture in Hunza: the wildest of high mountains, and a river valley culture, whose hanging gardens are cultivated between the giant peaks. It is like a paradise, a Garden of Eden on the roof of the world. Nowhere else in the world are there so many towering peaks in so limited an area.

The physical appearance of the people in Hunza is very different from that of the people in the rest of Pakistan. There is nothing oriental about them, they are light-skinned, often blond or red-haired, have light, often blue eyes and would not stand out at all in Europe. They like to describe themselves as the descendants of Alexander the Great's army. However, the origins of the Hunzakuts definitely lie further back. During the Indo-Aryan migration period the Persians left their "Aryan homeland" in the second millennium B.C. But some tribes remained behind, and today are still living in the Gilgit side valleys and inhabit the isolated highland world of the Pamir. Their connection with Persia can still be discerned today in religious rites – for example, fire festivals – and legends. Among the legends there is one which tells of two princes, who are said to have fled to Hunza from Persia with their followers around 1,000 A.D. The legend is probably based on the fact that at about this time there was very serious Islamic persecution of the Zoroastrians in Persia, as a result of which refugees from the Persian royal family may have retreated as far as Hunza. The language of ritual there remains Persian to this day.

---

23 11th century?

Ill. 44:
View of the Altit Fort from the KKH

Ill. 45:
The watchtower of the Altit Fort (before renovation)

The Hunzakuts also differ from the rest of the world because of their language: Burushaski is not related to any other language in the world, whether ancient or modern. According to Herrmann Berger[24] it is a highly developed language, which is the cultural equal of any other.

Burushaski is a tonal language. We were told that a single word can express a dozen concepts depending on the difference in tone. It took 20 years for a German linguist (Hermann Berger, see above) to produce a small dictionary of Burushaski.

It is assumed that the ancient Burushaski culture – to which Hunza belonged in antiquity – declined, with only the royal province in Baltit surviving. It is an almost untouched and unknown ancient world. In other mountain valleys remains of ancient cultures and peoples have also survived undiluted, but unlike the Hunza they are recognisably culturally connected to their neighbours. For example, there are the Dards who speak Indo-Iranian languages, such as Shina and Domaaki, or Iranian tribes who speak Farsi.

Cultic kingship survives in Hunza to this very day. The Mir[25] – the Hunzakuts call him "Tham", which is borrowed from the Chinese and means "Son of Heaven" – is regarded as being in harmony with the cosmic forces of nature. He dispenses justice, but is mainly responsible for working out the calendar and fixing the correct dates for the seasonal festivals. There are many elements derived from the Zoroastrian Mithras cult, but also Buddhist and Manichaean elements, as well as elements from the Tibetan Bön religion. Even though the Hunzakuts are Ismailis, their belief in Peri, the Great Mother, as well as fairies and demons, including a Hunza Pan, who frightens shepherds at night, plays a major role in their lives. These spirits inhabit what are called the pure regions above the tree line, which the shepherd, hunter or even the shaman may only enter after elaborate religious ceremonies. The shaman, the Bitan, is the most important man after the king. In a trance, he can leave space and time and travel into the past or the future, and also to heavenly realms, from which he brings messages from the Peri or the fairies as well as informing the Hunzakuts about future events. To fall into this trance, the shaman inhales the smoke from burning juniper twigs.

An important part of Hunzakut religiosity is their eating habits. The Hunzakuts only eat what they regard as pure and which transfers the power of

---

24 Professor in the South Asian Institute at the University of Heidelberg, who has written a lexicon and primer of Burushaski
25 Derived from Turkish "Emir"

growth from the plant and animal world unadulterated into their life. All food must be pure. This begins with the cultivation of grain, vegetables and fruit: the Hunzakuts find the use of artificial fertilisers or pesticides inconceivable. For example, in the spring the apricot trees are examined for pests and diseases, infected or damaged parts are removed or treated with a mixture of charcoal dust and glacier water. Individual foods are used as far as possible in unadulterated forms: thus corn is only ground shortly before use; they eat a lot of fruit, nuts and yoghourt; they use honey and dried apricots as sweeteners, as sugar was unknown until quite recently. The many and varied Asiatic spices, which could not have been unknown in Hunza because of their very old links with China, are also completely absent: they season their food almost exclusively with Himalayan salt. The Hunzakuts swear by glacier water, which they call glacier milk, as the fountain of health. It contains many minerals and traces of gold and iron. The Hunzakuts never drink with their meals, but only a few hours before or afterwards. Food is there for nourishment and not for pleasure. For cooking they press the oil from apricot[26] kernels: it is a very important part of Hunzakut food. It contains substances that are said to protect against heart disease, circulation problems and even cancer. The Hunzakuts fast for about one month in the year, in winter when all food except the seed corn has been consumed. This mode of nourishment, together with the pure air, the climatic conditions and physical activity, is probably responsible for the great age reached by the extremely healthy Hunzakuts.

At the end of the 19th century Hunza became the focus of interest of two great powers, Russia and Britain. The Russian desire to gain access to the Indian sub-continent by acquiring influence in Hunza made Great Britain, the colonial ruler in India, extremely uneasy and led to increased attempts to bring Hunza under British mandate.

Britain attempted by hook or by crook to persuade the Mir of Hunza to build a transport route from Gilgit to Baltit. On this subject Leitner[27] quotes an article from an Indian newspaper on the 29.11.1891:
"Col. A.G. Durand, British Agent at Gilgit, has received definite orders to bring the robber tribes of Hunza and Nagar under control. These tribes are the pirates of Central Asia, whose chief occupation is plundering caravans on the Yarkand and Kashgar. Any prisoners they take on these expeditions are sold into slavery. Colonel Durand has established an outpost at Chalt, about thirty miles beyond

---

26 Moreover the apricot is regarded as the woman's fruit, another example of the matriarchal principle.
27 Leitner, *Dardistan*, Appendix 1, p. 7f

Ill. 46: Our friend Sakit Ahmed (left) with his brother

Ill. 47: People in the Hunza Valley

Gilgit, on the Hunza river, and intends making a road to Aliabad, the capital of the Hunza chief, at once."

Leitner also adds, "They have absolutely done nothing to justify any attack on the integrity of this country; and before we invade it other means to secure peace should be tried."

The conflict resulting from British and Russian interests in acquiring power over Hunza almost led to war. It was only by a diplomatic agreement between Britain and Russia about the Pamir Knot that the contest known as the Great Game could be ended. At the Berlin Congress of 1878[28] Germany had ensured that Russia was compelled to withdraw from the passes north of Gilgit.

For the Hunzakuts, however, the period when they were the plaything of the great powers was a difficult time with major internal political confusion. Hunza's relationship with China had developed down the centuries: until the 20th century China had a mandate over Hunza,[29] without, however, ever having asserted any political claims to power. Hunza tried as best as it could to steer a course between the demands of the great powers without spoiling its position with China, which in the eyes of the Hunzakuts was their only reliable partner.

Internal political conflict for the throne to decide Hunza's external foreign policy led to murder and assassination in the royal house. Safdar Ali, who preferred an alliance with the Russian Tsar and the Chinese Emperor and was against any accommodation with Great Britain, decided the conflict in his own favour by killing his father and imprisoning his brother, until the latter agreed to swear fealty to him. In 1891 it finally came to a bloody conflict with the British. For the first time ever Ismaili Hunza and Shiite Nagar, who had been enemies since time immemorial, entered a military alliance. With 3,000 riflemen they jointly attacked the British and the forces of the Maharaja of Kashmir, who had annexed the Chaprot Valley in the west of Hunza at the end of the 19th century. Initially, the Hunza and Nagar troops were successful against an army that was numerically far superior to theirs.

At first the Hunzakuts and Nagars were at a great advantage: they could climb the steep cliffs with their rifles and attack the British from above. The British,

---

28 The Berlin Congress was an assembly of the great powers (the German Empire, Austria-Hungary, France, the United Kingdom, Italy, Russia and the Ottoman Empire) chaired by German Chancellor Prince Otto von Bismarck. The signing of the treaty on the 13th of June 1878 also ended the Balkan crisis.
29 Until the end of Manchu rule in 1912

for their part, were at a disadvantage in a terrain without the roads they needed to bring up support. And there were certainly no roads in the Hunza Valley. The British were forced to withdraw. They then founded the Gilgit Scouts with officers who had mountaineering experience. It was only when the British were able to match their mode of fighting to that of the mountain peoples of Hunza and Nagar that they were able to beat the Mirs' troops.

The British deposed Safdar Ali Tham and appointed his brother Mohammed Nazim Tham. Subsequently they also took over the Chinese mandate over Hunza. After reaching an agreement with the Russians about the Pamir Knot they ceased to interfere in the internal affairs of Hunza. They did not interfere with Hunza's autonomy or its cultic kingship. The development of the Silk Road to Karimabad, which the British had demanded so insistently, was abandoned after agreement with Russia was achieved. It was not until the 1970s that the Silk Road was developed by the Chinese by agreement with Pakistan – which now has sovereignty over Hunza – by means of the construction of the Karakoram Highway.

In antiquity there were three trade routes – Silk Roads – to the West. The most northerly passed through Samarkand, and the central one through the Oxus Valley, which 2,000 years ago led directly along the river valley to the Black Sea. We are now travelling on the old southernmost Silk Road. Marco Polo is said to have travelled to India along this route through the Hunza Valley. This old Silk Road was called the hidden road, the road travelled by the Sogdian merchants, Buddhist pilgrims and Manichean priests. It led via Gilgit to the cultural centres of antiquity like Bactria, Taxila or Peshawar, and also into the Swat and Kabul valleys, in this way becoming a pathway for the exchange not just of goods, but also of cultures. This trade route was also preferred by the Chinese for the transport of valuable goods, because it was more protected than the road over the open steppes. Even so, this route was also not without its dangers for travellers and caravans. The situation of places like Altit and Baltit was ideal for attacking caravans or demanding tolls for passing through. This "hidden" Silk Road was unknown to the West until the 19th century when it was first discovered by the British. Since the construction of the KKH it is admittedly easier to negotiate, but it still isn't easy, because nature is continually trying to block access to and transit through Hunza.

The Silk Road, which was given its name by the German geographer Ferdinand von Richthofen[30], was a network of caravan routes, some parts of which ran

---

30 1833-1905, Geographer, cartographer and explorer. In 1871 he travelled through Xinjiang.

alongside the Great Wall in eastern China. The different routes did, however, have one thing in common: the main routes all went through either Kashgar or Yarkand.

The period of the Silk Road's greatest importance lasted from about 120 B.C. until the 13th century A.D. Not only did trade goods like silk, spices and porcelain reach the West via this route, but religions, cultures and new developments in technology also spread along it. From the West to China the main goods were gold and other precious metals, glass and gemstones. In the West the most desirable product was silk.

The southern route, the so-called "hidden Silk Road", led from Xian in eastern China via Kashgar and the almost 5,000-metre high Khunjerab Pass, though also over the two more westerly passes of Mingteke and Kilik, through the Hunza Valley to the Indus Valley. The stretch from Xian to Kashgar meant travelling a good 2,600 kilometres – most of which was, in summertime, through boiling hot deserts. From Kashgar into the Hunza Valley the road was even more difficult. High mountains and snow-filled passes had to be overcome along narrow tracks hacked out of the rock. This southern Silk Road was given the name "Marco Polo Route" by the Hunzakuts and retains it to this day.

The roads passed through glowing heat and icy cold and were often so narrow that not even mules could be used as beasts of burden. Human beings had to carry the loads along footpaths. But the effort was worth it, because the Indus Valley at that time was the centre of a lively and varied cultural and spiritual life. This was the site of the high cultures of Taxila, Mohenjo-daro and Harappa, whose inhabitants were wealthy consumers of the goods that came from China. Some of the goods were – mainly along the Indus – transported as far as the ports on the Arabian Sea. For example, at Banbhore, 65 kilometres from Karachi, they discovered the ruins of an ancient harbour dating back to the first century A.D.

In the Banbhore Museum there is a rich collection of excavated goods which arrived there via the southern Silk Road: painted pottery vessels, coins, beads, glass, ebony carvings, pendants of all sizes and shapes with semi-precious stones from Europe. This many-branched network of trade routes reached the Mediterranean area even in pre-Christian times.

Only a few merchants accompanied their wares from east to west or vice versa. The few who made the whole journey were mostly travellers or adventurers, like Marco Polo, the Venetian who more than 700 years ago wrote a vivid account of his journey to the 'Middle Kingdom'.

Marco Polo was only 17 when he began his famous journey to China in the company of his father and uncle, who were both Venetian jewellers. When he returned to his home town in 1294 he was already 41.

Ill. 48: The Silk Roads

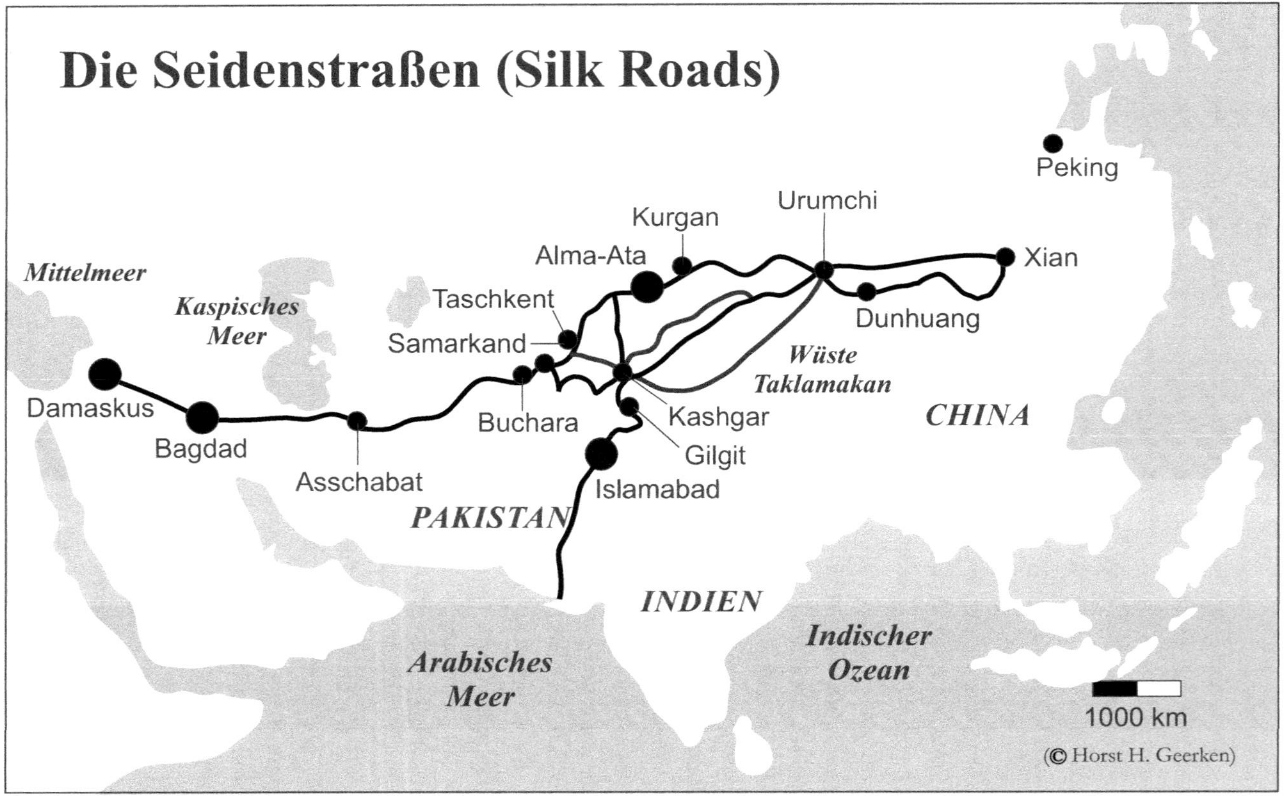

The goods were mostly handed over to intermediate dealers who transported them over a fixed stretch of the route. The Silk Road linked peoples of the most varied nations, religions and cultures. Tolerance was a major prerequisite for peaceful collaboration.

As during the course of the centuries long-distance trade shifted more and more to the faster sea routes and the trade in spices opened new markets in South-East Asia – mainly in Indonesia –, the Silk Road gradually lost its influence. When the Portuguese sailor Vasco da Gama discovered the sea route round Africa to Asia in 1497, it sealed the downfall of the Silk Roads. The failure of glaciers and rivers around the Takla Makan desert also contributed to their downfall. Without adequate water supplies once blooming cities and cultures disappeared.

Today the northern Silk Road route is known as the Heroin Highway, since this part of the Silk Road is used to smuggle heroin from Afghanistan to the West.

By now we've had a walk through the village, and as the crowning moment of the walk we drank Hunza wine under the counter of a Hunza shop – that is, the wine was under the counter, not us.

In an Islamic country this is unusual, but in the Hunza Valley wine has a very long tradition. The Hunzakuts were permitted to consume wine at the time of our visit. How much longer will this be so? We were invited into a private booth on the balcony. Since we arrived yesterday evening, Horst has been trying to develop friendly relationships with all our local neighbours in order to get at some Hunza wine – which is not supposed to exist. It took almost a whole day before he succeeded. We heard that the Hunzakuts do of course still produce their wine and drink it every day – but only within their own four walls. If they give it to foreigners or non-Hunzakut Pakistanis, they are severely punished. Wine plays an important role in Hunzakut worship and was originally mainly drunk during religious ceremonies. This is another connection with Zoroastrian belief. The Pakistani prohibition on the production of wine did not succeed in decreasing it, which the strictly Islamic Pakistanis are presumably well aware of. Hence the ban on serving wine to non-Hunzakuts.

As well as being invited to enjoy the wine in the shop, we were also invited into a Hunza home. We sat on the ground with the family, female neighbours came in and we were even allowed to take photographs of the women, which all our information had suggested is frowned on and forbidden.

Of course we also wanted to find out about the cultivation and production of wine, especially as the Islamic Pakistani government makes continuous attempts to ban wine. There are vines to be seen everywhere, growing beside the apricot trees, and these are the grapes the Hunzakuts use to make their wine. They press the grapes[31] by trampling them by foot. The juice is then led into a specially prepared reservoir in the ground, which is covered by a lid. In the middle of the lid is a hole covered by a stone. After about three months the wine is ready. The reservoir is opened and the wine is drunk with meals and especially at religious festivals. Wine plays an exceptional role in Ismaili religion. And we, of course, did full justice to the wine. It could not be compared with a Spätlese from Baden, but this natural, unadulterated wine was definitely drinkable. And it didn't produce headaches.

Before being invited into the Hunza home, we visited the Baltit Fort. Today it is a museum after being renovated a few years ago with funding from the Aga Khan and UNESCO. It is situated on the tip of a high rock, and the way up to it is very steep. It was built about 600 years ago, and at the time the Potala Palace in Lhasa is said to have been architecturally similar – influenced by the Gnostic traditions of the Manicheans. According to their legends, the realm of the priest-king Prester John is said to have been in central Asia and his residence to have been a Grail Castle made from the "great stone from the heavens": another reference to the ancient traditions of the cultic kingdom. The fort on the cosmic mountain is the ancestral castle of the Ayesho dynasty, whose members continue to be recognised as cultic rulers in Hunza to this day. In the lower floors there are dark chambers and passageways, spaces for business and for the soldiers who defended the castle with bow and arrow in times of crisis. Above, on the castle roof, from which there is a glorious view over Karimabad and the whole Hunza country, the Tham used in the past to receive visitors in private or public audience in a small, circular, columned hall.

Adjacent to the columned hall you can still see the private apartments of the Mir, from which he could watch polo being played on the polo field below the castle. The polo fields are generally at least as big as a football field. There is no seating for spectators. Houses and polo fields are mostly orientated west to east. Polo on horseback has a long tradition in Hunza, and in almost every village in the Hunza Valley you will find a polo field. Polo stars are greatly revered in Hunza, and polo offers every young farmer's son the opportunity to rise in society.

From our viewpoint up there we were only able to watch a training session: it was not a matter of winning. Nevertheless, the horses, with flared nostrils, were driven over the polo field by their riders, who seemed to be intoxicated by it all.

---

31 called *Djatsh*

During the period of British rule at the end of the nineteenth century the British learned the game from the Hunzakuts. They took it back to Britain, where it became very popular.

We were guided on our tour of the castle by the brother of the friend who had invited us to drink wine. A Pakistani family also took part in the visit with their little son, who to our astonishment spoke German to us. The father was an officer in the Pakistani army, where he had learned German, which was equally surprising.

The day has been so full of experiences. And yet we had not intended to arrive here until today. I can still hardly believe that I'm here. I can hardly take in all the new impressions. I often just stand and marvel at everything like a child in front of the Christmas tree. However, the weather is not playing along: it has been more or less cloudy for a week now, which is supposed to be unusual for this time of year. But we can still see the massive mountains, though not always in their whole majesty. So far it has really been a great trip.

Around Karimabad there are numerous water channels that you can walk beside at varying heights, because there is a path beside each channel to permit repair and maintenance. It was a delight to walk along these lovely, though narrow, paths and enjoy the beauty of the Hunza Valley. Since we were able to walk here for hours and were coping well with the altitude, we decided to take a trip to the Ultar meadows and the glacier. The path ran upwards beside a stream. After three hours, including a few pauses for breath, we were 1,000 metres higher. We came upon the gleaming white Ultar glacier beside a lush green meadow. What a sight! What a contrast! We were rewarded with a view over a wild but wonderful landscape. They say that masses of edelweiss grow on this mountain meadow in the summer and autumn.

Almost every minute gigantic avalanches broke away from the mountain and thundered down the steep slopes. A dramatic sight! In the middle of May the herds are driven up to the pastures, even to this mountain meadow beside the Ultar glacier.

The Ultar glacier at the foot of Rakaposhi – which is almost 8,000 metres high – is the main source of Karimabad's water supply. They are forced to use glacier water, because it hardly ever rains. The annual rainfall is less than five centimetres.[32]

---

32 On 2015, the average *monthly* rainfall in Oxfordshire in the UK was three times as much.

Ill. 49: View over the Hunza Valley. Along the irrigation channel something green is growing.

Ill. 50: At the baker's

After an hour we had to tear ourselves away from this uniquely delightful view because we wished to be back in Karimabad by daylight. For Annette the descent was much more difficult, because her back was causing her problems. With my help, we managed to get back to Karimabad in four hours. We were happy to have survived the trip in good heart and proud to have achieved it. The following day was rather more restful – because of very stiff muscles – and so we abandoned a planned trip to a mine where they dig for rubies.[33]

So far I am coping well with the altitude. Yesterday Horst was panting a bit on the way up to the Baltit Fort, but fortunately it has passed today, though it can change from place to place. Tomorrow we're off to Gulmit, which is a bit higher than Karimabad.

I'd actually intended to post some things today, but since it's a religious festival the post office is closed. I assume it's the same religious festival that causes so much conflict between Sunni and Shia that we had to leave Gilgit early for safety's sake. During the night there was loud drumming and singing, which then continued all day. But we didn't actually notice anything except women carrying large dishes of food somewhere and the incessant singing.

Today we walked to Altit, which is a good three kilometres from here down in the valley, and where the old fort of the Mir is situated. It is about 700 years old, so around 100 to 200 years older than the Baltit Fort we visited yesterday. The Altit Fort is a fortified building on a steep rock 300 metres above the Silk Road. Unlike the Baltit Fort, the Altit has not yet been restored and so is gradually falling into ruin, which is a great pity[34]. A boy of about 12 guided us and explained some things about the fort in quite good English. It's surprising how few people in Pakistan speak English these days, even in the major cities.

Horst climbed boldly around the crumbling parts of the fort, which made me weak at the knees just to watch. Fortunately he drew the line at climbing the extremely ruinous tower, which he would have had to climb into by means of a quite rotten looking window. When we tried to give our young guide a tip at the end of the visit, he refused categorically and just scampered off. I found that quite surprising as well.

We had intended to eat lunch in Altit, which unlike Karimabad looks much more authentic, but unfortunately there was only tea. Food was only served

---

33 In 2000 the Karimabad/Baltit Region region won the World Award of Tourism in competition with Indonesia, Australia, India and Great Britain.
34 In 2009 the Altit Fort was restored with help from the Aga Khan Foundation.

in the evening, and we didn't want to wait that long, so we made our way back to Karimabad. In Altit we met a procession of singing women who were carrying a very varied selection of food to a ceremony in a house, but we were unable to get any more information about what it was. Our return journey was another glorious walk, because there was not only the magnificent view of the landscape, but today the sun also shone all day and a cool wind was blowing.

Here in Karimabad everything is, as I said, much more touristy. There are several guesthouses and small hotels, and way down in the valley even a 5-star hotel,[35] so of course we had to go and look at it. The hotel belongs to the Mir and was completely empty. They offered us a 70 % discount on the price of the room and a free evening meal to tempt us into the hotel, but we could not be persuaded. Even when the manager threw us a "you-could-do-with-a-hot-shower" look – and he was completely right –, we did not weaken our resolve. To be the only guests in a great lump of a building like that, was a horrible idea. Not even the offer of hot water could change that.

Up in Karimabad the electricity supply is quite complicated. There isn't any at the moment! The generator of a small hydro-electric power plant is out of order, and so there is no hot water either. Being tough (or wishing to be so) we take a shower in ice-cold glacier water with much moaning and groaning, rejoicing and congratulating ourselves afterwards on our bravery. We only asked once for two buckets of hot water to wash our hair. In the evening, as soon as it is dark, the generator is switched on, but it cuts out immediately because it is too small and is, therefore, overloaded. Then we sit in darkness. By now we have fortunately acquired candles from our host, so that we don't have to feel our way clumsily through the darkness. At 9:30 p.m. the generator is finally turned off until the next evening, and then all the guests have to go to bed. Our technical expert Horst naturally wants to give his opinion on the subject of electricity as well:

Pakistani switch-mania:
Pakistani hotels seem to measure their importance by the number of electrical switches in the bedrooms. Wherever we went, in all the hotels, even the most simple, whole batteries of electrical switches were fitted, the function of which remains a mystery to me even now.
In the World Roof Hotel in Karimabad the set-up of the switches was very confusing. There were four switches near the entrance to the room, eight on the wall

---
35 5 stars by Pakistani standards!

Ill. 51:
Over the roofs of Altit

Ill. 52:
A view of the upper Hunza Valley

near the beds and two further switches at the head of the beds. During both our stays in Karimabad there was no electricity, because the channel bringing water to the little hydro-electric power station was blocked and the generator itself was damaged. However, in the evening the World Roof Hotel switched on a small Honda generator, though we could only switch on a single lamp.

This switch madness ran like a common thread through every Pakistani hotel room, giving us constant cause for laughter. In Dasu we found seven light switches for a single light bulb, and in another place a switch for "Room service". Even though we initially hadn't even found this switch (and if we had found it, the idea that it would ring a bell somewhere would never have entered our heads), a boy kept arriving, claiming we had summoned him by the bell. Perhaps another room was connected with our bell.

Another example: in our room in the Hunza Inn in Gilgit there was a large switchboard set into the wall with a sign saying "Danger! 430 Volt". Next to it there were two rows, each of ten switches. In this room it was relatively easy to work out which switch was which, since over two of the switches there was an L for Light and over another one an F for Fan in red paint. The other switches were only there for decoration, but you could play with all 20 without any danger since there was rarely any current and we always had to sit there by candlelight in the evenings. The way into the bathroom, where there was also rarely any running water, passed through a "Vestibule" with a wardrobe, a chair and a bare light bulb hanging from the ceiling – but there was an impressive row of six light switches, as well as switches for a non-existent ceiling ventilator and a non-functioning bell. There was no painted L here, so that you had to play on all the switches like a piano to find the right one for the light – if there was any current, that is. I couldn't understand where the 430 volts were coming from since, to judge by the brightness of bulbs designed for 220 volts, the current was at most 130 volts.

Today, the 8th of May 1998, there's electricity again, but only for half an hour, and then we sit by candlelight again, waiting for it to return. That, on the other hand, could take another half hour or more, so nothing much has changed from what we had with the little hotel generator. Except that the hot water is supposed to be back on with the return of the current.

After writing some postcards we went to the post office, which is directly opposite our hotel and is reached by a flight of very steep high steps, which I was later only able to get down with Horst's help. We spent half an hour sticking on stamps[36] before we finally set out on the way to Ganesh.

---

[36] Note from January 1999: And then I didn't watch the post office stamping process carefully enough so that 50 % of the cards never arrived!

Ganesh lies about 2.5 kilometres below Karimabad, right beside the Karakoram Highway. Here we took a long walk along the KKH: all traffic had been brought to a halt by a major landslide.

Ill. 53:
Alone on the KKH

Ill. 54:
The road into the Hopar Valley

6. The Hopar Valley

During our walk from Karimabad to Ganesh the driver of a jeep asked us if we'd like to go to the Hopar Valley. This high mountain valley is another 1,000 metres higher than Karimabad, at an altitude of a good 3,500 metres. The valley floor is several hundred metres higher than the peak of the Zugspitze, the highest mountain in Germany! The valley, which lies in the Nagar area hostile to Hunza, is praised for its special beauty. Unlike the Hunza Valley, the people there are fanatical Shiite Muslims, and are said to be quite hostile to foreigners. However, we did not wish to miss the chance to go.

After a bit of negotiation about the price, the jeep driver was prepared to take us there for 1,000 Pakistani rupees.[37] We got him to lower the jeep's canvas roof so that we could see as much as possible, and off we went. First we crossed the Hunza River and then hurtled along beside the Nagar River at a more than brisk pace – hurtled as fast as was possible! A glance upwards – the driver, of course, was keeping a constant eye on the steep mountainsides – made it clear to us just why he was speeding. You could see from the many large and small boulders on the road, and also from the mountains themselves, that the road is in great danger of rock falls. The driver wanted to put the dangerous stretches of the road behind him as quickly as possible. Then we crossed the Nagar River by a suspension bridge, and from here onwards the danger of rock falls was over. But then the road began to climb – it was now a very narrow dirt track – so steeply that I was in constant fear that we might fall sideways into the valley below, or that the jeep wouldn't manage the gradient. The ideal road for people with as little head for heights as I! Though I must say that I have become far less prone to vertigo, presumably since I have climbed Angkor Wat in Cambodia (more pushed and shoved than under my own steam), and now as a final test of nerve driven along the Karakoram Highway. Even so, I felt quite uneasy on several occasions when a whole piece of the road had fallen away, or when a vehicle came from the opposite direction, which fortunately only happened twice.

The journey up into the Hopar mountain valley was breathtaking and picturesque. The people in the roadside villages were mostly friendly and waved, though a few children threw stones.

Hunza and Nagar, which are separated by the Hunza River, have been enemies since time immemorial. The Hunzakuts are 98 % tolerant Ismailis,

---

37 about € 25/£ 20

Ill. 55:
Nagar

Ill. 56:
The path to the Hopar glacier

while the Nagars are fanatical Shiites. A few years ago, when hostilities flared up, they even burned down the bridge that links Hunza and Nagar over the deep abyss of the Hunza River. Our driver was from Nagar, which obviously made our journey safer. His brother, who is a policeman, travelled with us a part of the way. I had also, as I always did, wrapped my sarong around my head. It is good protection against the sun, but in Islamic, particularly in Shiite, areas it also always makes a good impression, and you can see that they look on you in a more friendly way. And so we travelled through a magnificent mountain landscape into the Hopar Valley.

The season was far less advanced here than in the Hunza Valley: we were, after all, a good 1,000 metres higher. While in the Hunza Valley the apricot blossoms were already past, here they were just beginning to flower. In Hopar we had reached the end of the road that could be travelled by motor vehicle. The village consisted of farms that were spread out, far from each other. A young man immediately offered to guide us to the Hopar glacier.[38] We first enquired about lunch, and were told that when we'd been to the glacier, there would be dhal, potatoes and chapattis waiting for us.

So we set off for the glacier first. Oh my goodness! I may by then have acquired a somewhat better head for heights, but this was a desperate venture for me. The path ran along a very steep slope, with a precipitous drop at the side, and in places only a foot wide. Even so, I did manage half the distance – though I was sweating profusely. But then I kept on slipping and decided to strike when we reached a place where a quite large rock offered a good sitting place, so that I had a good view of the glacier and the snowy giants all around. Two of the boys from the village came to keep me company until Horst returned from the glacier. I only let Horst go under the strict threat that if he fell to his death I would have him taken back to Germany and, as a punishment, buried with the greatest possible pomp and ceremony! That seemed to me to be the best way to keep him from doing anything foolhardy. In spite of this, he walked off in high spirits and could soon only be seen as a tiny dot far beneath me. I watched the glacier at my leisure – it really is alive! It creaks and cracks continuously, stones that are lying on it fall off, and you can see that the ice is in perpetual motion. The glacier is said to move over 20 centimetres a day. It was relaxing to watch it from a safe distance.

I was, however, delighted to see Horst and the guide when they appeared safe and sound again in the distance far below us. The two boys who had stayed with me had tried – with a great deal of effort – to explain all sorts of things about the glacier, the area and their village. Beyond the glacier, a day

---

38 also known as the Bualtar glacier

or two's journey away, there are other villages, but they can only be reached by crossing the glacier, and very rarely come into contact with the Western world by means of trekking tours. They tried to point out a farmer who was bringing his produce across from over there and was still on the other side of the glacier, but I could not see him. However, so as not to disappoint them too much, I claimed that I had managed to do so. They also said that it was quite easy to cross the glacier; you only had to know the right places and avoid the crevasses. I'm not so sure: given the way the glacier is moving, today's "right place" could mean your death tomorrow. So I felt no desire at all to undertake the adventure, especially since first I would have had to climb all the way down to the glacier!

In fact I had enough trouble getting back to the village. But going upwards is far less problematic than going downwards. It was just at the very narrow places that I grabbed at any hand that was offered me, and when we were finally back at the top I was very happy and proud of myself.

At the place where we had started our hike a table and two chairs had already been set up, and we were given our lunch accompanied by native tumurru herbal tea, a mixture of mint, coriander, jasmine, green tealeaves and other typical Hunza Valley herbs that we were unable to identify. The food tasted wonderful, but not only did they demand an outrageous price for the meal – it also made us ill. What we could not know at the time was that we would experience the 'joy' of this meal for the whole of the rest of our trip – and even months later in Germany my stomach and intestinal tract were still not back in order.

With a great deal of trouble and suffering great distress we just managed to get back to our hotel before a bad attack of diarrhoea set in. The potatoes and vegetables had doubtless been cooked in glacier water. Since we were at an altitude of over 3,500 metres, the boiling point of the water would have been only about 80°C. Certainly, not all the bacteria would have been killed. Nor did we know how long the food had been cooked at 80°C. I should have thought of that before the meal. It is hardly surprising that the potatoes were still quite hard. After the meal I also had problems for weeks.

We then drove back along the same route – there was no other choice. We would have liked to visit the Mir or Tham of Nagar, since the Rosinys, who knew him well, had asked us to give him their regards, but unfortunately he happened not to be in the country. On the return journey we particularly noticed the speeches of the mullahs, which were being broadcast everywhere

*Ill. 57:
This meal at an altitude of 3,500 metres in the Hopar Valley kept us "happy" for quite some time.*

*Ill. 58:
Back to Karimabad*

from the mosques by loudspeaker, and sounded extremely fanatical and aggressive. Even in Hunza on the other side of the river and the deep gorge you could hear the speeches from early morning onwards. We almost felt that the loudspeakers were being provocatively directed straight at Hunza. It is thus no surprise, that the ordinary population is incited to such an extent that it leads to bloody unrest.

Towards 4:30 p.m. our jeep driver, who was really very nice and considerate, dropped us at our hotel. For the last stretch between Ganesh and Karimabad he drove us along the old Hunza road, which is so steep that you really feel you are driving vertically up into the sky. All we could see was the bonnet of the jeep and the sky. Everything here is mountaineering, even on four wheels!

Back in the hotel, we were admittedly ill because of the food in the Hopar Valley; we were also dog-tired and totally shaken, but still extremely enthusiastic about our wonderful day out.

7. From Karimabad to Gulmit

The morning after our trip to the Hopar Valley we wanted to get on our way towards Gulmit. At the time the road was said to be still blocked by a landslide which would only be cleared in a couple of days, but it was said that you could climb over it and find some kind of transport on the other side. We wanted to see for ourselves. On our journey to Karimabad a similar landslide had been reported, but had been cleared by the time we arrived.

By now, on the 10th of May 1998, we have arrived in Gulmit and are sitting in the garden looking out over a heavenly mountain backdrop, enjoying life. We're just noticing how beautifully spicy the air here smells, but that is the spicy scent of the tumurru tea we have just been brought. This native herbal tea is exquisite: all the herbs come from far up on the mountain slopes. But even without the aroma of the tea the air up here at 3,000 metres is fantastic. And the tranquillity is unbelievable. We are really completely cut off from the frenzy of civilisation.

Gulmit is a village on a high plateau between the most tremendous mountain massifs in the world. We've ended up here in a small guesthouse, the Hunza Marco Polo Inn, where – as we thought – the Rosinys have been before us. Everyone remembers Mister Tonny and his wife. Mister Tonny from Lahore was a very good friend and spent a month here with his wife and two daughters about eight years ago. At this point I began to be perplexed: Mister Tonny from Lahore was strange enough, since Herr Rosiny lived in Islamabad, but two daughters into the bargain: something wasn't quite right. But we didn't let our surprise show, because as acquaintances of Mister Tonny, even if it was the wrong person, we would be better received than any old tourists without a recommendation.

But let's begin at the beginning: yesterday morning was the first time we didn't have to shower in ice-cold glacier water, but – because there had been temporary current for a few hours the evening before and our boiler was still warm – in warm water. Somehow we missed our refreshing ice-cold showers and our loud shrieks of terror.

We set off on the road to Gulmit in a jeep. We knew that the road was supposed to be blocked, but were very much hoping that the blockage would

Ill. 59:
On the road to Gulmit

Ill. 60:
Annette crosses the landslide with multiple help

have been removed by the time we got there. The fact that no cars were coming towards us and that we were about the only people travelling towards Gulmit seemed a bad sign to me. And in fact, about 20 kilometres from Karimabad[39] that was it! Gigantic boulders were piled metres high on the roadway. The whole landslide was, as Horst later told me, 100 to 150 metres wide. Some locals and an explosives detachment of the Pakistani army were clambering about on the rock fall high above the road. On our side, there was a queue of cars waiting for passengers from the other side. A small bus arrived at the same time as us, full of tourists who wanted to see and photograph the landslide. When we unloaded out luggage from the jeep, some of them came over to us and asked if we really intended to climb across there. We said that we would at least try. I felt like a real daredevil as I said so! Nothing at all could have made me turn back now, but I didn't look any more closely at the landslide, so that I wouldn't fill my pants in terror beforehand. Our driver carried my holdall: he was coming across with us to negotiate a good price for us on the other side for our journey to Gulmit. Horst also gave his rucksack to a porter, so that he could help me.

Just before I reached the landslide I began to feel very uneasy, but when an elderly gentleman from the tourist bus asked me if I was really serious about climbing across, the question was finally decided. I would at least have to try. The gentleman clapped me on the shoulder, wishing me good luck, and I got Horst to help me up on to the first of the boulders. The first twenty to thirty metres went relatively well, but then the soldiers suddenly shouted: "Go, go, go, fast, fast," and blew loud blasts on their whistles. All I had heard was that the soldiers would signal with their whistles shortly before detonating their explosives, so that you could retreat to safety. On the first part of the climb I had seen the fuses of the dynamite charges hanging out of the rocks. I panicked and thought, "They really are going to set them off, even though they ought to know that we haven't reached the other side yet." At the same time I had got into a situation where I could not move either forwards or back: I had my feet in the wrong position, one foot on one boulder, the other foot on another and was clinging for dear life to another one, but in a way that meant that I couldn't move. I thought, "That's it, it's the end, they're going to blow me up!" What I – perhaps fortunately – didn't realise was that the whole rock face above us had started to move and was about to crash down on us. Horst dashed impulsively back to me, a local arrived from behind me – he had kept close to me the whole time, as I had noticed from the corner of my eye. With his help I took a leap into

---

39 Gulmit is about 40 kilometres from Karimabad

the unknown – I still can't believe that I dared it –, and landed on the rock where Horst was standing and caught me. From there I sent Horst on ahead and got the local to help me onwards – they all climb up and down over the most difficult tracks and rocks. I was still unaware of what danger we were in, although I had a feeling that the rocks were moving beneath us – though I thought it might be just my trembling knees –, and the soldiers were still shouting, "Go, go, fast, fast." The local did not leave my side and only let go of my hand once, when he himself started to totter; apart from that, he helped me from boulder to boulder in spite of the danger, always encouraging me to hurry, though very patiently. I never once looked down, because if I had dared to look down into the depths, at least 150 metres below, I would probably not have moved an inch forward. I just concentrated on my next step. I was not aware of anything, not my legs, not my arms, I was exclusively focussed on taking one step after another, while beneath my feet the mass of debris slid away downwards.

Horst remained a few metres ahead of me the whole time, so that he could rush to my aid again if necessary. Suddenly he shouted, "This is the end!" I literally hopped over the next boulder to Horst and from then on it was child's play. It was only then that I discovered why the soldiers had been so anxious to encourage us to hurry, but it took a while to sink in that we had missed being crushed by the mountain by a hair's breadth. When I finally reached safety, Horst took me in his arms. We were both quivering all over because of the anxiety and effort, our eyes filled with tears and we hugged each other tight. The whole unstable rock fall was on the move again and slowly slid away. This crossing had been a really hazardous undertaking!

With our driver's help we found another jeep on the other side and bargained a good price. And after a heartfelt farewell from our driver and other helpers – sweetened, of course, by a fair-sized tip – we continued on our way to Gulmit.

Today I'm really stiff all over, but I have noticed that the roads in the Hopar Valley and above all the scramble over the landslide have made me less subject to vertigo. Here in Gulmit I am already hopping up- and downhill almost like a chamois – admittedly a rather clumsy chamois, but still a chamois!

In Gulmit we have landed on our feet in the Hunza Marco Polo Inn. Gulmit, a small, really old, picturesque village of mud and stone huts, is a fair reward for all our trouble. It is really fabulous here. The alleys between the houses are only about a metre and a half wide, and the people are incredibly

Ill. 61:
Our Hotel,
the Hunza Marco
Polo Inn

Ill. 62:
The bridge into the
Shishkat Valley

friendly. They all greet us and wave, and we are constantly being invited into the houses for tea. Apart from us there are no tourists anywhere in the vicinity. This morning we spent three hours exploring the village and its surroundings. Yesterday, the day we arrived, we only took a little a walk, apart from which we just sat in the garden and read, recovering from the shock of the landslide. We let our amazingly beautiful surroundings work on us. I really can't stop raving about it: the massive snow-covered giants, most of which have still not been climbed, the lovely valley full of flowers, the isolated village life and the extremely nice people. Ever since we've been in the Hunza Valley, I've kept thinking that it really is just like being in paradise. No wonder James Hilton was inspired to write his novel about Shangri La here. But I wouldn't like to be here in the winter! Although the winters are supposed not to be so severe here because of the south-facing position and the powerful direct sunlight. We did notice, however, that spring in Gulmit, because of its higher altitude compared with Karimabad, was lagging behind by about two weeks. Because of the mild winter even tropical fruits like oranges are said to thrive in Karimabad.

But now back to our walk. It is the first absolutely cloudless day since we left Islamabad. The sun is very strong up here,[40] but the air is very clear and cool, so that it is wonderful for walking. In the mornings and evenings, however, you need thick pullovers, and at night we are well-wrapped-up with bellybands, scarves and ski-underpants! Not very becoming, but practical. Today we wanted to look at the "footbridge" into the Shishkat Valley. To do so, we had to go along the KKH for a stretch and then climb down a steep slope to the Hunza River. With my recently acquired experience of mountaineering and landslide climbing, that was no problem for me. I even skipped off ahead most of the time! But the bridge – no! A team of ten horses couldn't have dragged me onto it, let alone across it. It's a swaying suspension bridge about a hundred metres long, with struts only every half metre. Never mind my experience with the landslide, this wasn't something I wished to become acquainted with. No need to go overboard with tests of courage! But nothing could stop Horst, certainly not rational arguments: he had to go onto the bridge, and said it was child's play! But even that assurance couldn't tempt me to indulge in this pleasure – and the bath in the Hunza River that would no doubt follow! For my sake he didn't cross the whole bridge as far as the entrance to the Shishkat valley – and still regrets it deeply even today, at the end of December 1998.

---

40 The Hunza Valley is at the same latitude as southern Italy.

It is really picturesque here, and today we've shot more than one roll of film. Both Gulmit and Karimabad are surrounded by glaciers which shine gleaming white in the sun. There are dozens of glaciers around here. Tomorrow we want to stay here, and then start our journey to Kashgar, where we want to spend a good week before returning here for a few days more.

This evening another acquaintance of Mister Tonny was brought to see us, a Mister Khan Beg. Mister Khan Beg is a mountain guide with whom Mister Tonny went trekking and hunting, apart from which Mister Khan Beg visited Mister Tonny in Germany for two months. His flight and everything else had been paid for. He had drunk a lot of alcohol, Mister Tonny had always been so generous and they had had so much fun. He had also visited Mister Tonny in Lahore, and Tonny's daughter had been a great help to him. When Mister Khan Beg then asked after Mister Tonny's mother, I, without hesitation, declared her dead. By now it had become clear to us that we were dealing with another family called Tonni or Tonny – even though Horst kept asking me if I was really sure that the Rosinys had no daughters –, and so I had no qualms about burying the mother, which was not all that unlikely eight years after Mister Tonny's last visit.

Today, the eleventh of May, we're a bit out of it. Tired, short of breath and a bit faint. But that could be because we both woke up at 3 a.m. today because we were so excited. We had both woken up, each of us thinking about what we should pack for China – because we want to take only one small rucksack between us – and what we should wear on the journey. We were also pondering on our dreams. It was only when we needed to go to the loo that each of us realised that the other was awake too. So we shortened the night by talking and laughing a bit, and for our further amusement Horst played an imaginary fiddle and I completed the artistic feast with a display of ballet. The final artistic touch was provided by our clothing: long ski-underpants, belly bands, scarves and rubber flip-flops.

We fell about laughing, forgetting that, to our annoyance, a German family – parents and a daughter – had moved in for a night the previous day and were sleeping in the room to our left. After our show they probably were no longer asleep! Since we were still wide awake and worked up at 4 o'clock we each took an opipramol tablet to relax us so that we could get at least a little sleep. That's probably what left us so washed out today.

The German family that trolled in here yesterday evening could have been as nice as pie, and perhaps we would even have liked them somewhere else,

Ill. 63:
The staff of our hotel. Second from the right is the owner of the hotel, the petty tyrant Raja Hussein Khan, looking very grim as usual

Ill. 64:
Tea time in the hotel garden with a view of the Golden Peak

but not here! We wanted to be alone in the place. But I suspect that we wouldn't have wanted any contact with them anyway. The daughter was massively built, as was the father, though the mother was normal size. The daughter seems to be working somewhere in Pakistan. We discovered that when the hotel owner talked to her about her headgear – she was wearing a brightly coloured Hunza woman's cap –, and said that she looked like a Hunza woman, to which she answered that she had suffered from sunstroke in the Hunza Valley a month before. That of course explained why she never took the cap off, even indoors and at meal times. But if she was here a month ago, then she is probably not a normal tourist. In the mean time they have left, and we're happy again.

Now we've packed our things for China, and realised once more that half of the luggage we've brought would have been enough. But that's always the case, you always take too much "just in case".

Today a family invited us to take tea in their house; of their six children the two youngest sons are severely physically and mentally disabled. There are a striking number of more or less mentally and physically handicapped people here. I assume it is because of in-breeding. The individual villages have been so cut off from the world for centuries that, even though marriage within one's own clan is not permitted, the clans have become so closely related because of intermarriage that it is no longer advisable to intermarry.

Given the arrogance of three Englishmen who have just passed through – the KKH was open again today after seven days of blasting and clearing work –, I've begun to think that it's also inadvisable for the English to intermarry within their small island. We're glad that they travelled straight on.

At the moment it's raining, which makes the road towards Gilgit – that is, the opposite direction to the one we're travelling– very likely to have more landslides. After yesterday's dream weather today's rain can't affect us at all. We're just glad to see the Pakistanis standing in the rain, because we hope that it will give them some kind of a wash – something they obviously do very sparingly here. Of all of them, our host smells extremely unpleasantly of unwashed clothing, but none of the others are much better. In spite of this, they are all incredibly nice and helpful.

Our host, Raja Hussein Khan, is at the moment playing "mother" to us: he organises and deals with everything without asking us first. He has organised two tickets for our journey to Tashkurgan in China,[41] ordered two

---

41 In Tashkurgan we have to spend the night and then continue our journey in a Chinese bus.

lunch packets, he'll take us to Sust, where the bus for China leaves from, and will presumably also make sure that we're sitting in the right seats on the right bus. It's very likely that he'll deal with the passport formalities for us as well. He's also threatened to organise our journey back here from Sust: he's already told somebody that we'll be returning to Pakistan sometime next week, and they should then presumably pick us up in Sust!

At the moment promising smells are wafting from the kitchen: they're preparing our dinner. Our cook, Hassan, comes from Karimabad and can – as he says – cook anything! So far he's been right, although our demands were not excessive. What we want more than anything is Hunza cuisine. Admittedly he does look a bit scruffy, smells like all the rest here and keeps scratching himself in intimate places,[42] but until now we have had no problems with his food, even if all his apricot dishes are loaded with sand. He has just informed us that in about four weeks' time fungi will burst from the ground everywhere, wonderful edible fungi. In Karimabad they would eat them, he said, but here in Gulmit people would trample on the fungi and never dream of eating them.

We have made the "Restaurant", the hotel dining room, into our living room, where we write, drink tea, and read when it is too windy or cold out in the garden or – as it is doing now – rains. From here, as from the garden, there is an excellent view over the Hunza Valley up to the snow-covered mountains.

After dinner we had another encounter with Shah Khan, the proprietor of the Silk Route Hotel, who was in a state of mental inebriation resulting from excessive alcohol consumption. Horst had already visited his hotel when we were looking for accommodation in Gulmit.

Down by the KKH, right on the edge of the road, is the Silk Route Hotel, which was given its name by Herr Rosiny. The day before yesterday, when we arrived, I inspected the rooms and the beds and enquired about the price. The whole hotel was empty, all the rooms were simply and sparely furnished, but relatively clean. The price for a double room was 1,150 rupees. After negotiation with the manager in his suit, shirt and tie, I got it down to 800 rupees. Still far too expensive, and so I made him a final counter-offer: 500 rupees and not an anna more. "No! No! Not possible!" But when I turned to go he called after me, "Okay, I give you single room charge for double". I turned back in delight to find out the price. He offered 798 rupees, 2 rupees less than his previous offer. I'd had enough, and

---

[42] I suggested: "Don't scratch, wash!"

Ill. 65:
The garden in the Hunza Marco Polo Inn

Ill. 66:
A chance encounter

Ill. 67: The school in Gulmit

Ill. 68: Another encounter

we went away and drove to the Marco Polo Inn, where, with the aid of the false Mister Tonny, we were comfortably and cheaply accommodated.

And now the proprietor of the Silk Route Hotel is standing before us: Mister Shah Khan, jovial, drunk, in a tailored suit like a British colonial official, a silk cravat round his neck and a brandy bottle sticking out of his pocket. He was also enthusiastic about meeting friends of Mister Tonny (I'm sure he meant the right Mister Tonny), but paid no heed to the finer distinctions in his jolly, alcohol-befuddled state. He tried very hard to cajole us to drink, but we refused, because we didn't want to sacrifice our own good whisky in return! There was no way of stopping his torrent of speech, and, delighted to have visitors from Germany in front of him, he told us about his experiences in Germany, where he had been stationed as an officer in the Royal Air Force. The best part of that had been the German Fräuleins! They'd all been so beautiful and cheerful.

Tomorrow morning we're off again, to the Khunjerab Pass, almost 2,000 metres higher than here, and today we're sitting around like two flopping fish, exhausted, no strength and panting for air. It looks as if it'll be fun! Even the short walk to the post office was difficult for us. Perhaps in my case that is because no letters from Germany and Australia have arrived in the Gulmit Post Office yet. It all takes so much longer here. I couldn't get the postal official to understand what poste restante means, and so I sent the owner of the hotel, Raja Hussein Khan, to find out for me. Now we can only hope that when we return in about a week there will be some letters there.

Today the sky is cloudy again and there is a strong wind blowing. We went for a walk along a few kilometres of the KKH. It's all peaceful, no traffic: the KKH is still – or once more – blocked towards Karimabad. The road has been blocked for seven days now, and all we saw was a queue of about 20 lorries which were waiting for the road to be cleared. The KKH can't be that busy if so few vehicles have been held up.

Yesterday evening, one day before the full moon, we saw a beautiful moonrise – twice within 15 minutes. We saw the first moonrise from the polo field, which is high up. It was fascinating to see how the bright disc of the moon rose behind the nearby steep mountains in Nagar, bathing everything in bright, blue light, in which we and everything else cast long shadows. The long glaciers gleamed in the moonlight and reflected the pale light back. The atmosphere was spellbinding. We walked down the narrow path to our hotel, and as we did so the moon slowly vanished behind the mountain massif and around us everything became *dark. Then we were lucky enough to experience a second moonrise from the hotel garden, as everything around us was bathed more and more in the mystical light of our earth's satellite. We were surrounded by a sky of black satin and a mighty snow-covered mountain world in resplendent moonlight.*

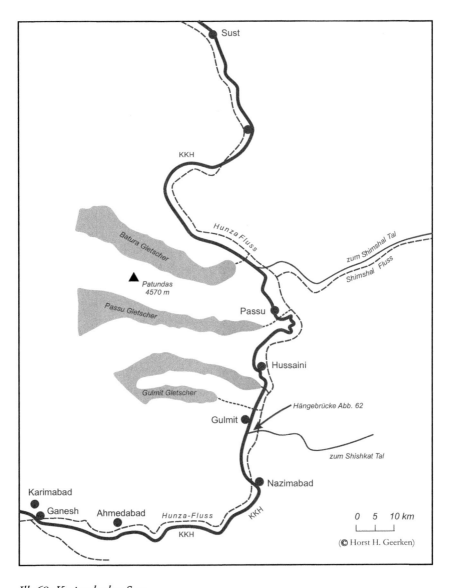

Ill. 69: Karimabad to Sust

8. From Gulmit to Sust

We reached our goal, Kashgar, yesterday evening, the 14th of May. What a journey! On the morning of the 12th we set off for Sust. For our journey there our host placed a newly bought – 1981! – lorry at our disposal, though we both had to squeeze in the front with him. Of course, the lorry had to be properly initiated into the family, which meant preparing a feast. For this purpose – while we were eating our breakfast – a goat was slaughtered in the yard before our eyes. Enjoy your meal! A good start to our journey. If the butcher had been guided by his sense of smell alone, he might well have slaughtered our host!

Our host didn't accompany us to Sust since he was expecting an important visitor that day, but he placed us in the trusty hands of his brother. After about 20 kilometres we passed Passu, which is an unremarkable place, though until a couple of decades ago it was of great strategic importance. This is where there is the turn-off across the Hunza River into the Shishkat Valley and where the paths from Ladakh, Xinjiang, the Pamir and Afghanistan meet. The paths through the Mingteke and Kilik passes to Xinjiang, the most important passes before the completion of the Khunjerab Pass, also branched off here. The approach of foreigners and enemy hordes was always detected first in Passu and reported to Karimabad.

The brother's help was also necessary, because without aid from a local we would still be wandering around in Sust today. In this small collection of buildings there were only customs and immigration offices, a post office, a place where bus tickets were sold and several shabby dives which they called 'hotels'.

The first thing the brother did was to take us to a hotel in Sust; we were somewhat in the dark as to what we were supposed to do there, until we were asked if we had ordered a packed lunch. But since it was impossible to look at the interior of the hotel without shuddering, and we were completely nauseated when we used the loo in one of the rooms, we immediately said no, even though we were well aware that our host, in his infinite concern for us, had ordered a packed lunch. Judging by the state of the hotel we could well imagine what the kitchen must look like. The only thing that was okay about the room we had seen had been the roll of loo paper, which we immediately requisitioned. The toilet itself was in such a terrible state that we fled, leaving it unused.

*Ill. 70:
Another 55 km to Sust and 136 km to the Khunjerab Pass. China is getting closer!*

*Ill. 71:
It keeps on going upwards*

We had anyway already sorted out our travel rations ourselves, having bought two packets of Tuc biscuits and some apple juice in Gulmit. Two rations of biscuits, two bottles of apple juice and some spring water to dilute the juice would be enough to survive the two day journey to Kashgar. We were, however, also presuming that we would get something to eat in Tashkurgan that evening. Since we didn't want the packed lunch – the explanation that we don't eat meat was good enough – the brother took us to the bus station. We'd already asked him while we were in the horror hotel if we shouldn't go to the ticket office, but he said it was much too early. When we finally arrived at the ticket counter we almost had to apologise because we were the last there.

Then, when we had the tickets, the chaos began, total confusion at the bus station: people, buses, tied up luggage everywhere. Someone had told us that we would only be travelling with locals on the bus, but there were also two Americans on the list: I looked around for them. There was only one man who looked a bit like a Westerner. He had fair hair and was wearing jeans and a jeans jacket, but was travelling with four cats and an old lady, who with her headscarf and her entire mode of dress did not look at all Western – but not Pakistani either. Needing, as I do, to assign a history to everyone, I decided that they must be Americans, who had emigrated there some time ago and were now visiting their homeland – wherever that might be. But it was still difficult to fit the cats and the piles of luggage into my story. But I wasn't given much time to think about it, because I suddenly had to consider my own physical well-being and find a half-way clean toilet somewhere.

The 'brother' had assigned a Pakistani to us, who accompanied us the whole time and helped us through the chaos. The 'brother' himself had to greet and chat to people all the time and was probably above such menial tasks. After several requests, this Pakistani set off with me to find a reasonably clean loo. Horst came with me as well, as a precaution. We left the bus station cross country, jumped over a drainage ditch, luckily avoided falling into the sewage and arrived on the other side of the road at a 'hotel', where our Pakistani minder after a certain amount of negotiation handed me over to one of the hotel boys. He led me to a room that was obviously occupied by at least three people. Two used beds with clothes on them and a mattress on the floor which was also strewn with items of clothing and other travel equipment. So that I could get to the loo at all, the mattress was hoisted up, all the contents fell on the floor and I was shown the way to the loo with a lordly gesture. It was reasonably clean and it was most important to me to relieve myself as much as possible before our long journey.

Then our minder took us back to the bus station, which had by now become much more crowded with travellers, who were obviously returning from the Hajj to Mecca. Now Horst also needed the lavatory, and had seen something that looked like one in a corner of the bus station and classified it as a loo, because women kept rushing over to it and on the way were already unbuttoning themselves and lifting their skirts. When we asked a weighty and important-looking official if that was the loo, the only answer we got was "Out of order". Horst, however, did not let himself be distracted, but went over and relieved himself somehow in the place, which was in an indescribable state. The important looking official obviously felt that his honour as a state servant had been attacked and complained angrily to all the other officials who were standing around, though obviously the only thing I could understand was "Out of order". "Good grief," I thought, "when we go and get our tickets registered, he'll simply tear them up, since we're now *personae non gratae*."

But then another of the officials came over and offered me a chair, which calmed me down. By now we had been standing in the bus station for an hour in front of a table with a chair on either side, where officials with lists of passengers kept sitting down, but then standing up and going away again, and nothing happened. Our bus, we were informed, had not yet arrived, although we should actually have been on our way for an hour by now.

Suddenly something did happen: our passport numbers were entered in the passenger list and our luggage was registered. I realised that this had nothing to do with checking in, but was simply Pakistani customs control. The angry official – who had surely thought that you couldn't trust even the Germans any more if they ignore instructions about things being 'out of order' from a uniformed official – couldn't tear up our tickets after all. After customs registration our minder led us out of the bus station once more, along a market street, over a building site, to another corner of Sust, which was where passport control took place. When the passport official saw that we had a visa for two single entries into Pakistan, he was overjoyed and explained to us that we would surely be extremely happy to be allowed to return to Pakistan, and bade us farewell by saying "Welcome to Pakistan", even though we were actually on the point of leaving.

After completing the Odyssey back to the bus station, we found that our bus was actually there. A rather swish, medium size bus, and our seats were right at the front. The gentleman with the cats had already boarded, and so had his mother. The bus was only two thirds full, and, therefore, very comfortable. Gradually the other passengers got on and, an hour and a half late, our journey could begin.

9. From Sust over the Khunjerab Pass to Kashgar

We were well wrapped-up because we were aware that the Khunjerab Pass is at an altitude of almost 5,000 metres and it can get very cold there. The mountain landscape was impressive in its grandeur as the bus wound its way ever higher up the road. It was breathtaking, but very different from what we had experienced on the KKH until then. So far the bus had run beside a rock wall above the Hunza River the whole time, which always looked very threatening and frightening. Now the road became more open, and the bus spiralled up the mountainside. According to Horst the road was very like that over the passes towards Leh in Ladakh.

We are here amid the Karakoram range, with peaks of up to 8,600 metres. The mountains are black, all around there are heaps of black gravel deposits, so it is no wonder that this range acquired its name: in Turkish 'kara' means 'black' and 'koram' gravel.

This is where the Indian plate collides with the Eurasian plate as it shifts north. The Indian plate continuously presses under the Eurasian, causing regular displacement. These tensions are resolved in powerful earthquakes and consequent rock falls. For example, the earthquake on the 8th of October 2005 cost around 75,000 lives in Pakistan and India. The Karakoram Range is constantly in motion.

The highest mountain in Karakoram is K2, at 8,611 metres the second highest mountain in the world. If you cast your gaze around, you see a concentration of more than 60 mountains with an altitude of more than 7,000 metres. Everywhere in Karakoram you come across one of the more than 50 glaciers. At a length of up to 70 kilometres these are the longest glaciers outside the polar regions. Karakoram is of great interest to geologists and glaciologists.

We suddenly remembered that we had forgotten to take our panacea, aspirin – in this case for altitude sickness –, and quickly remedied the situation. When we were at the top of the pass – at almost 5,000 metres and nearly 2,000 metres higher than the Zugspitze – we felt fine. Whether that was because of the aspirin, or because we had gradually worked our way slowly up to ever greater altitudes from Gilgit (about 1,800 metres) to Karimabad (about 2,500 metres) and on to Gulmit (about 3,000 metres), I am not qualified to judge. Still, when we ran, quickly and without permission, through the barrier to the Chinese side because we had seen a lavatory on the other side of the border, we were quite out of breath from the run and our hearts were pounding.

Ill. 72: Karakoram, the Black Mountains

Ill. 73: At the top of the pass, the border with China

The border post is a rather miserable affair, consisting of a kind of large portakabin standing alone and lonely in the bleak landscape. One could well imagine the border guards quickly dying of boredom so far from any kind of civilisation. And yet borders always have something special about them. A few thoughts from Horst about this, inspired by the Indonesian travels of Karl Helbig:

The fascinating thing about borders is the way they always exert a special attraction on people, even though they are just dead lines and the other side of them mostly looks just like this side. But to know that those rocks up over there are in China gives you a very extraordinary feeling. Here the border is nothing physical at all, simply an imaginary concept in unoccupied space: for dozens of kilometres on either side of the border there is not even the smallest human settlement. The top of the pass is quite level and long. On the Pakistani side there are ruins: the former accommodation of the Chinese road workers.

At our request the bus stopped briefly at the border stones that are at the highest point of the pass, only a few kilometres before the border post with its passport and customs controls. I wanted to take a few photos, because the Swedish explorer Sven Hedin and the German Adolf Schlagintweit had stood on this historic spot before me. One would expect some kind of memorial to these great explorers and to the fact that we are here in the centre of the Pamir Knot, but all there is is a stone commemorating the opening of the pass in August 1982.

All the male Pakistanis used the stop to pee on the Chinese border stone. This was meant to express their low opinion of China, and was accompanied by general merriment. The first Chinese road sign also looked like a sieve as it had been used by the Pakistanis as a target for shooting practice.

When we drove on, we had to move to the other side of the road: traffic drives on the left in Pakistan and on the right in China. Then we had to move our watches forward. That caused great confusion: some said it was one hour, others that it was four. We couldn't even solve this problem at the border post with the help of the border officials. In their isolation they live without clocks or any sense of time.

Then we had to deal with Chinese passport and customs control, which in this total isolation from the rest of the world took place in the middle of the road. We'd got a visa for China in Bonn, but there was still a great palaver, because it's most unusual for visitors from the West to enter by this border crossing. They finally let us through but with strict instructions that we must go through another control in the chief customs office in Tashkurgan. The main thing was that we got through.

Ill. 74: Chinese border post

Ill. 75: Customs control at an altitude of almost 5,000 metres

All the luggage had to be unloaded from the bus, and Horst was just assuring me that as foreigners we wouldn't have to open our luggage anyway, when there I was squatting in the middle of the road and was invited to unpack our holdall right there under the vigilant eyes of a Chinese official – everything in it! And I insisted on showing him everything, even the things he didn't want to see. He kept saying, "Okay, okay," but I went on mulishly unpacking, even opened the sewing kit, the toothpaste, the sun cream, all the while explaining to him with hands and feet and in German what it was all for, while he was forced to squat and watch. Horst stood beside us adding his tuppence worth in Swabian dialect.

The American with the cats was the one who was searched the longest, and all sorts of things came to light: saucepans, ladles, sleeping bags, in short a whole household in four gigantic holdalls. Horst had already learned a bit about him in Sust while I was in the loo. He was not actually born in America, but an immigrant from the eastern bloc, Siberia apparently. He had lived in America with his mother for seven years and then moved on to Greece, which is where two of the cats came from, then Macedonia (1 cat) and after that to Syria (cat no. 4), and now he and his mother with their four cats were on the way back from the various stations of their life – we assumed – to Siberia, because she thought it was the best place for her, and also not so hot. We presumed that they might be gypsies, because they had also lived a while in Rajasthan in India. When he too had finally been dealt with and all the luggage stowed in and on the bus and tied fast, the barrier was raised for us and we were able to head off past a row of saluting Chinese officials for our next destination, Tashkurgan, about 160 kilometres away.

Shortly after crossing the border we saw our first 'picturesque' sight: an Uyghur – as I deduced from his hat – with a camel! Very artistic, but unfortunately we passed by so quickly that there was no time for a photo – the greatest delight of tourists who wish to impress their nearest and dearest back home. Then, a little bit beyond the border, the landscape changed considerably. It looked exactly like what I imagine Outer Mongolia to look like. There were even the nomad yurts with camels and herds of goats and yaks. I was quite excited, because I'd always wanted to go to Mongolia, and now it was as if it was there before my very eyes![43]

The closer we got to Tashkurgan, the drier the landscape became, the yurts disappeared and there were more and more permanent dwellings, farms built of mud which fitted into the landscape so well that you sometimes had to look twice to make them out.

---

43 In 2005 this wish was fullfilled. We crossed the Gobi Desert in Mongolia together.

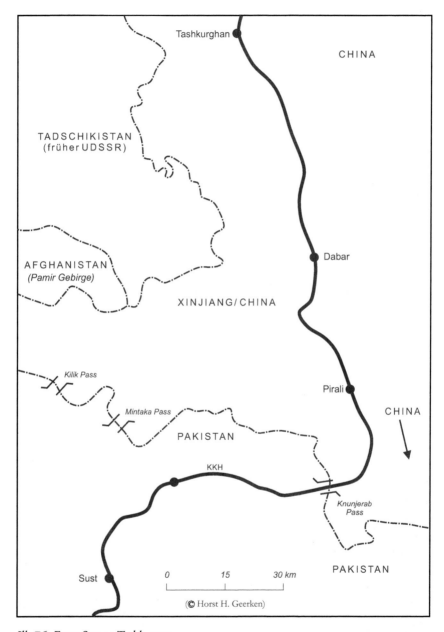

Ill. 76: From Sust to Tashkurgan

Ill. 77: Yurts in a desolate landscape

Ill. 78: On good roads on the Chinese high plateau

The farms are surrounded by mud walls, and when the road passed above them you could see that there were several inner enclosures, probably for the inhabitants and their animals. They are presumably completely dependent on raising animals, as the area is too barren for agriculture. It's almost unbelievable that people can live there at all. I could hardly imagine any sort of existence being possible in this barren gravel wasteland, but that is obviously a fallacy. We drove through several minor tornados, which whirled dust and sand up into the air and increased our sense of the inhospitable nature of this area. Camels, horsemen and farmers with wagons drawn by donkeys proved to us again and again that the area was inhabited.

We reached Tashkurgan, which is at an altitude of 3,700 metres. I've never seen such a miserable dump. It consists of just one street about three kilometres long, with more or less dilapidated huts and a few larger buildings on either side. First, however, we had to go through passport and customs control once more, as we had been warned: it went very smoothly. Then we changed some money into Chinese currency, because we had to buy our tickets for the journey on to Kashgar straight away. A Chinese woman in uniform was standing beside the money-changer, who also provided our tickets for the journey onwards – twice as dear for foreigners as for the Chinese. And yet in real socialism everyone is supposed to be equal! With the almost unintelligible words "This bus will bring you to your hotel", she ushered us over to a bus.

And there we were, sitting alone in the bus, which didn't take us anywhere, but just stood there! So long that Horst finally set off to find out why we were not leaving the spot. He found the bus driver and the Chinese woman asleep in the customs building. When he woke them, we did actually move on.

But the bus didn't take us to the Pamir Hotel, which we had actually chosen, but to the Traffic Hotel, right beside the bus station, where the Chinese woman informed us categorically and in a tone that brooked no contradiction, "This is your hotel!" According to the guidebook and some Japanese people we'd met en route who confirmed what the guidebook said, there is never any water there and the loos are full before you even arrive! No wonder: it's a state hotel where negligence and laziness reign.

We got them to show us a room, and since we're not over-picky we decided it would do for just one night. Apart from a spanking brand new television set it was horribly run down and the bathroom was a catastrophe. There was no water, of course, but the Chinese woman assured us that it would be running in ten minutes. Horst threatened that we would demand our money back if that didn't happen. And after ten minutes there was actually running water, though only in the washbasin.

And so we stayed in that dosshouse, also because the Traffic Hotel is right beside the bus station from which our bus would leave for Kashgar the next morning. To get to the hotel we had chosen – the Pamir Hotel, number one in the town, though the Traffic Hotel was supposed to be the number two –, we would have had to walk about a kilometre with our luggage, since there are no taxis or other transport facilities in Tashkurgan. And the next morning we would, of course, have had to walk all the way back. Since it was quite difficult to find out when exactly our bus was supposed to leave, and whether that would be by local unofficial time,[44] it was also important not to be too far away from the bus station. There was great confusion about the right time! And so we installed ourselves here just to be safe.

Then we set out on a search for dinner, since apart from a frugal breakfast – since our experience in the Hopar Valley we had had stomach and bowel problems – we had eaten nothing and by Pakistani time it was by now late afternoon.

In our hotel there was nothing anyway, and along the miserable street we didn't discover anything that appeared even partly acceptable. So we walked to the Pamir Hotel, visiting Tashkurgan's only sight on the way – the fort that stands on the town's only hill.

But in the Pamir Hotel there was no food either, since there were no guests. But they kindly showed us a room, which wasn't exactly the tops, but was several classes better than the Traffic Hotel. For our return journey, they issued us with a VIP card so that we would come back to stay there, which we also intended to do. They also advised us to go and eat in a restaurant called 'Mohammed's Restaurant'. However, we were unable to find it, and since no one on the street could understand us, we bought two bottles of beer, carried them back to our scruffy room and enjoyed the beer with one of our two packets of Pakistani Tuc biscuits. We thought they tasted great, and we felt completely full and happy. Except that two bottles of beer weren't enough for us, and so we marched off to buy some more bottles, which we did in a little shop in the Icefall Hotel diagonally opposite, a small hotel whose rooms are not that bad at all, except that they don't have en suite bathrooms.

---

44 Local unofficial time: 1 hour earlier than in Pakistan; official Peking time: 4 hourse earlier than Pakistan

Ill. 79 and 80: Tashkurgan

In the shop we met up with our Pakistani bus driver, who had driven us from Sust to Tashkurgan. He was completely plastered, and so delighted at our reunion that he insisted on inviting us to help him down any number of alcoholic beverages. As a good Muslim one has a duty at least to try to remove this devilish brew from the world. But we just declined, bought our bottles of beer and then continued our walk a little.

On this walk through Tashkurgan, which really gives the impression of being the end of the world – it seems like a former den of thieves –, we did actually find Mohammed's Restaurant in a back courtyard, and it was really nice. No one understood us, but they took us straight into their very clean kitchen to choose something to eat. When we left because we were already full they were all disconcerted, and we were really sorry to disappoint them in this way, but we undertook to eat there on our way back – as long as we had no stomach problems at the time.

Against all expectations we even slept well in our second-best hotel. The beds were admittedly not very well maintained – I can hardly believe that they were regularly changed: it's hardly worth it since most travellers only stay there a single night –, but we always have enough sarongs and our own pillows with us, so that we don't have to come into contact with the bed-clothes at all.

But we did have to put up with some nocturnal disturbances when the 'housekeeper' on our floor suddenly tried to stick a completely roaring drunk Pakistani in our room. In China you don't get your own room key, you always have to use the floor staff. Our 'housekeeper' was a constant source of delight to me with her transparent frilly nylon dress and red high-heeled shoes, on which she keeled over every second step. When she tried to put the drunken guest into our room, we shouted so long and so loud that they eventually left our refuge.

After that we barricaded the utterly hopeless door with our clothes stand and a thermos flask. In the night there was yet another disturbance when someone else tried to get into our room, but the noise of the thermos flask and clothes stand falling over put the intruder to flight immediately.

Then in the night I suffered a little from shortness of breath because of the altitude, and because Horst was sleeping so peacefully I suspected that he had probably died from lack of air. But instead of checking straight away, I began to think desperately about where I could have him cremated in an Islamic country and where I should strew his ashes! As I became more and more worked up about the problems I saw heading towards me and felt that I was getting less and less air, I finally managed to decide to use the flashlight to see if my deliberations were at all necessary. And, lo and behold, he was sleeping deeply like a baby. So I thought, anything he can do I can do too, forgot my breathlessness and very quickly went back to sleep.

Annette was simply feeling that she wasn't getting enough oxygen. As a result of my experiences during a trek of several weeks through the equally high Zanskar Valley in western Tibet,[45] I knew that you should lie with your feet a bit higher than your head at night. This means that your brain has a better blood supply and you don't have difficulty breathing. When I was there I always pitched my tent so that my legs were higher than my head.

In spite of Annette's friendly, but dubious, comments I went out to the hotel yard in the evening to look for things suitable to raise the foot of my bed that night. I found two bricks and brought them back. Annette could not be persuaded to do the same! That might well be the reason why I slept so well.

The next morning there was no breakfast in the hotel. We refreshed ourselves royally on our habitual travelling drink, consisting of water with a dash of apple juice and some of our second packet of Tuc biscuits. And then off we went. This time in a totally overfilled and clapped-out Chinese bus. This was where we once more bumped into the people returning from the Hajj in Mecca, whom we had already seen in Sust, in the vanguard a really malevolent witch, who caused disruption from the very start. Apart from us the only foreigners in the bus were two Japanese and an Englishwoman. One of the Japanese and the Englishwoman were sitting in front of us in the bus, and the Englishwoman was immediately snarled at by the witch when the latter tried to put a canister of water – presumably some kind of holy water from Mecca – right in front of her feet and the Englishwoman said no. Good grief, how that witch could rant. At the same time, she bagged two seats for herself, probably because she was coming back from the Hajj and didn't want a man sitting next to her. That meant that some men had to sit on the floor.

The bus left nearly an hour late. Horst and I had managed to arrange ourselves somehow on the very narrow seats, on which according to the timetable we were going to spend seven or eight hours. In this bus there were three seats on one side of the gangway and on the other side – where we were sitting – only two. The seats were, therefore, quite narrow. We were sitting half on top of each other, and if one of us wanted to change position, the other had to do so too.

---

45 Ladakh in northern India

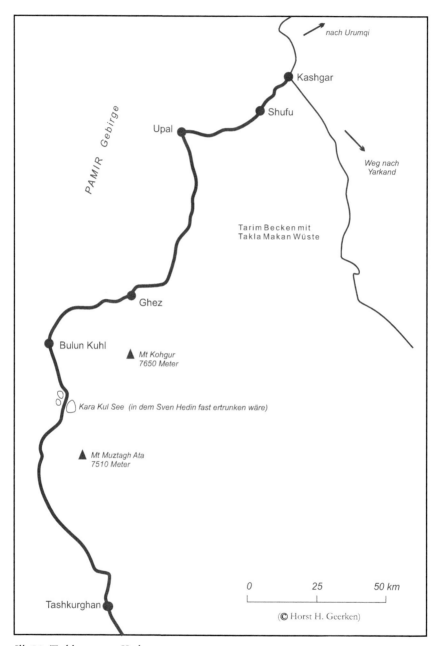

Ill. 81: Tashkurgan to Kashgar

Our journey went on through a fantastic region. Great high plateaus surrounded by glacier-covered mountains, a landscape totally different from the one that the KKH runs through on the Pakistani side. On this high plateau, the Subash Plateau, you come quite near to the Afghan and Tadjiki border which runs through the Pamir mountains. It is also possible to cross the border there, but it has so far been forbidden for tourists. The Subash Plateau is a bit higher than Tashkurgan, and the bus could only creep laboriously up the mountains because – as Horst said – engines do not get enough oxygen at that altitude. But after a while it began to go almost constantly downhill and we travelled on more quickly. The road here was very good. A stream wound its way through the plateau, and on its banks enough vegetation was growing to feed the herds of yaks and goats.

After a few hours we reached Lake Karakul, which seemed to Sven Hedin, when he arrived there, to be like a paradise in the Takla Makan desert, and in which he almost drowned. It is really beautiful to see the snow-covered mountains reflected in the deep blue water, and there are even a few simple yurts where it is possible to spend the night. But you never know when you are going to be able to get transport from there, and for that reason we had not included a stopover in our plans. The closer we came to the plain, the Tarim Basin, the more barren the landscape became, and yet there were still some isolated farms.

Sven Hedin, born in Stockholm in 1865, was a Swedish geographer, explorer and travel writer, who made three expeditions to Central Asia and the regions beyond the Himalayas between 1893 and 1927. His first expedition ended dramatically. Several of his companions and the camels died of thirst in what was called the Todeslager [death camp]. He described this expedition in his 1898 book 'Through Asia'.

His fourth and last expedition in 1935 took him back to the Takla Makan desert in north-west China, the second largest desert in the world, which borders on the Gobi desert to the east. Sven Hedin was probably the first European to cross the heart of the Takla Makan, the Desert of No Return, whose extremes of dryness and devastating sand storms make it the world's most life-threatening desert.

The 1935 expedition was undertaken under the auspices of the German Reich. It was intended to explore the possibility of a flight connection between Germany and China for Lufthansa. For the aircraft of the period it was necessary to find places where water and refuelling facilities for intermediate landings were available.

As early as 1926 the first exploratory flight took place with two three-engined Junkers G 24 aircraft. In 1934 there was also a successful flight from Berlin to Shanghai via Moscow – the shortest route – in exactly four days using a single-

Ill. 82: Lake Karakul with Muztag Ata (7,510 metres) to the south[46]

Ill. 83: Lake Karakul with Mount Kohgur (7,650 metres) to the north[47]

---

46 https://commons.wikimedia.org/wiki/File%3AKarakul_Lake_-_Muztag_Ata%2C_China.jpg

47 https://upload.wikimedia.org/wikipedia/commons/c/c5/Mt_Kongur_Lake_Karakul_China.jpg

engined Junkers W 34. In the same year a Junkers Ju 52 flew the longer route to China via India. For political reasons, the most important of which were internal Chinese turmoil and the difficulty of getting permission to fly over British India and Russia, these routes were no longer available. However, the German economy required a flight-connection to the Far East, and so the only route available was that via Greece, Rhodes, Syria, Iraq, Iran and Afghanistan over the Hindu Kush and the Pamir mountains to China.

In 1936 there was a first preparatory and exploratory flight from Kabul over the Hindu Kush and the Pamir mountains in a Junkers Ju 52. They had Afghan air-force officers and German aviation meteorologists on board as well as the crew. After reaching Chinese territory the aircraft turned back, returning to Kabul. In order to acquire exact observations of the quickly changing weather conditions in the Hindu Kush and Pamir mountains, a weather station was set up in the most remote region of the Pamir with the permission of the Afghan government.

After Sven Hedin had explored the route via western China and his reports had been evaluated, there was a successful flight to China with two Junkers Ju 52 under the command of Carl August Freiherr von Gablenz. The first aircraft had the registration D-ANOY. Supplementary tanks were built in to the cabin. The second plane was to take off a week later. The section of the route that is of interest here went from Kabul via the passes in Pamir, Hunza and Xinjiang. The flight path passed to the north of Gilgit and the northern Hunza Valley, via Tashkurgan to Yarkand, which was their first landing-place in China. From Yarkand, which is near Tashkurgan, the flight continued to Chotan[48] and then over the Takla Makan desert to Xian in eastern China. Yarkand and Chotan were part of the Chinese mandate territory in what is now Xinjiang, near the north-eastern end of the Hunza Valley which at the time belonged to Hunza.

The return flight followed the same route. They had to make an emergency landing at Lob near Chotan, an oasis on the edge of the Takla Makan desert, because of engine problems. Marauding Turkmen and Chinese hordes captured the Germans and imprisoned them in the citadel of Chotan: war had broken out between various warlords in the Chotan region, and no end to the conflict was in sight. The warlord who was calling the tune in Chotan took the Germans' passports away: they were never returned. During their involuntary stay in Chotan the crew were able to see the lodgings in which Wilhelm Filchner – of whom more later – had been imprisoned for half a year only a few months previously. By now the crew of D-ANOY had spent almost four weeks in captivity and there was no indication of when they might be allowed to leave. They began to make plans to travel to British India with a caravan via Tashkurgan and through the Hunza Valley.

---

48 now Hotan

The Hunzakuts of Yarkand and Chotan had already provided assistance to Sven Hedin, Wilhelm Filchner and Peter Fleming[49]. Now they also intervened to help the airmen. A makeshift runway was prepared which, since Chotan lies at an altitude of 1,400 metres, had to be correspondingly long. After an adventurous take off, D-ANOY flew over the Pamir Knot once more. The updraught allowed the aircraft to reach an altitude of 6,500 metres in spite of its spluttering engine. The crew were constantly forced to take a breath from the oxygen bottle. The mountains were partly covered in clouds: the pilot had to guess where they were as he was flying blind – and with a failing engine. Suddenly the sun broke through and the clear weather allowed a view of Nanga Parbat. When they returned home, they said that it was the loveliest flight they'd ever made. D-ANOY, down to its last drop of fuel and with a juddering engine, landed in Kabul after a successful flight. They were invited to stay in the German Ambassador's residence, and their families were informed that the whole crew was safe and sound.

For four whole weeks D-ANOY and its crew were regarded as missing. In Germany the Reich Aviation Minister immediately instituted a search. Firstly, two Junkers Ju 52 were sent, reaching Kabul in only 28 hours. A third aircraft was equipped for long-distance flight and followed later. One search mission after another was carried out. They flew over the Hindu Kush, the Karakoram and the Pamir mountains again and again. Without success. They presumed that the aircraft had crashed in this region. It was, in fact, only a little further east on the edge of the Takla Makan desert near Yarkand und Chotan. They also sent out search missions from the east, from China, but because of the military situation the search teams could not get as far as Xinjiang.

The crew wanted to return to Germany as soon as possible. The juddering engine was repaired as far as possible, but during the flight oil consumption increased so much that they had to change aircraft at Teheran. They returned to Germany via Baghdad and Rhodes, landing at Tempelhof airport in Berlin on the 3rd of October 1937.

It was a daring and pioneering achievement, reconnoitring a new air route to the Far East over the 'Roof of the World'. Von Gablenz, leader of the mission and pilot of the aircraft, describes the flight in a most interesting and exciting way in his book 'D-ANOY bezwingt den Pamir' [D-ANOY Conquers the Pamir]. Today, in 2016, D-ANOY can be seen at Munich Airport.

In 1935 and also during the Second World War Sven Hedin was received several times by Hitler and other leading National Socialists, which is strange, since

---

49 Author of: *One's company: A Journey to China in 1933*, 1934 and *News from Tartary: Journey from Peking to Kashmir*, 1936

Hedin was of Jewish descent.[50] *Because of this closeness to Hitler and the Third Reich, Hedin was ostracised in his homeland, Sweden, after 1945.*

Lake Karakul, mentioned by Annette above, was formed by a meteor impact about ten million years ago. At an altitude of 3,650 metres it is one of the highest lakes in the world. It is surrounded by several snow-capped peaks of 7,500 metres, which are reflected in the clear, glassy waters of the lake. Glaciers wind down the mountains into the desert. It is an impressively beautiful landscape.

On one occasion we came to a Chinese checkpoint, where we all had to get off the bus to show our passports, and there stood several women with dishes full of bread and boiled eggs. None of the travellers dared take the bread even though it didn't look bad at all, but they all stuffed their pockets full of eggs. For safety's sake, we eschewed these culinary delights as we still had some biscuits left.

Horst wanted to empty his bladder and rushed off towards the loo. However, the Pakistani who had been travelling with us since Sust and giving us a constant flow of information about the region brought him to a halt with the words, "Better outside!"

Fortunately I did not have to rely on these sanitary facilities, since an hour before – again at the instigation of our Pakistani – the bus had made a comfort stop in the middle of the road in the open countryside. The men lined up right on the edge of the road, and I just stood there, not knowing where to go. Then I saw a Pakistani woman vanishing behind a quite large boulder which I had failed to see in the monotonous landscape. I thought if it's good enough for one, it's good enough for two and pushed my way in beside her, to which she did not object. She had also travelled with us from Sust, and since she was travelling alone her husband had asked me if I would sit next to her. But the problem was solved by the fact that on this bus there were single seats for just such cases.

The Pakistanis, who travelled with us, were all businessmen who lived by trading with China. They presumably came from Gilgit or even further south. They travelled to Kashgar with practically empty bags, then bought household goods, silk, wrist-watches and other useful things there, filling their bags with them. After a few days they would then arrive back in Sust, where the customs office was. Apparently it is possible to get through the customs control there quite cheaply in return for a little baksheesh. In Sust they hand their goods over to a

---

50 Eric Wennerholm, *Sven Hedin – En Biografi*, 1978, p. 304f

Ill. 84: Our road through the lonely desert

Ill. 85: A small caravan

Ill. 86: A small village

Ill. 87: How is it possible to live here?

middleman, and everything is sold at a profit in Pakistan. They then set off for Kashgar again the next day with empty bags.

After the checkpoint we drove through the mountains for another hour, but then the weather steadily worsened. At first we thought that we were entering a rainy area, but it turned out to be dust. It got darker and darker, so that we had only a vague view of the mountains. We began to think that there must be a very big sandstorm somewhere if the air was so dusty here. Then we reached the plain, the Takla Makan desert, and after half an hour we knew exactly where the storm was: we were actually in the middle of it!

It was incredible! At first I was quite excited, because I had never experienced a sandstorm before, but the excitement didn't last. At first the bus could only travel at walking pace, but then it couldn't move at all. You could literally not see two metres in front of you. It became black as night, red or white, depending on the colour of the sand that was hitting us at any particular time. Even inside the bus you could hardly see a thing because the fine sand came in through every crack. We could hardly get any air and everyone was coughing alarmingly. Horst and I pulled our sarongs over our heads and so were better protected than most of the others, but the fine sand penetrated even our sarongs, and we too were forced to cough, trying to breathe only through the nose as much as possible. It lasted for hours, and it got increasingly difficult to breathe. The noise of the sand blasting the bus was indescribable. At first the Englishwoman in front of us moaned and groused because the bus wasn't driving on, though it was a complete mystery to me how it could have done so. But eventually she gave up because all she could do was cough and not talk. We got ready to spend the night there, and were glad that shortly before the storm we'd eaten a couple of our biscuits and had been careful with our water.

After more than five hours the storm finally subsided and against all expectation we suddenly continued on our way. About time, because we'd had more than enough of those hard, narrow seats. When we unwrapped ourselves from our sarongs and it was possible to see a little better inside the bus everyone looked the same: grey! Faces, hair, clothes and luggage as well. Even we, who at first had been saved by the protection of our sarongs, became visibly greyer, because the dust was still swirling around in the bus and the storm outside had by no means stopped, just subsided a little.

But these hours of waiting had aroused aggression. Suddenly there was a disturbance behind us: the malevolent witch had spat at a Chinese man, who had spat back which in its turn caused one of the men travelling with her to grab him by the hair. Not to be outdone, the Chinese man punched him a couple of times – and the witch as well. Horst and the Pakistani, who had been chatting to us the whole time and was obviously annoyed by the old witch, cheered on the Chinese man. Then one of the people from the front of the bus stormed to the back and gave the Chinese man a slap in the face. At the very moment that the passengers in the bus began to divide into two camps and threatened a mass brawl, the soldiers – who could only be distinguished from the grey mass of passengers by their headgear – intervened and brought the glorious spectacle to an end. Finally, to the delight of all parties, the bus driver stopped on a stretch of open road and threw a couple of passengers out because they had apparently not paid. That could not have been anything new for the driver, however, since he had picked them up on the way and until then hadn't even asked them for any fare. This action calmed the angry crowd somewhat and the journey could continue.

Not long after that, and thirteen hours after our departure, we were in Kashgar. In the bus station, to the general amusement, we took off everything we could without causing a public nuisance. We shook out all our clothes to get rid of at least a little of the sand that was sticking all over us. After that we found a taxi and drove to the Seman Hotel. We had finally reached the end of the KKH.

When we got out and saw the outside of our bus, we hardly recognised it. In Tashkurgan a large part of the Chinese bus was painted in red and blue. Now the bus was gleaming silver. Even the smallest traces of paint had gone. The sandstorm had scoured the bus completely bare – and at no cost at all – as if it had been sandblasted. And that's how we arrived in Kashgar.

10. Xinjiang[51]

After leaving the Khunjerab Pass behind us, we have entered the Chinese province of Xinjiang, which is nearly seven times as large as the United Kingdom. The term Central Asia encompasses the geographical and historical area which was earlier known as Chinese Turkestan or East Turkestan. One wave of invaders after another flooded the region until China finally succeeded in conquering it in the second half of the 18th century, although it was never totally integrated into the Chinese empire. From 1884 onwards East Turkestan was called Xinjiang, which means 'New Province', by the Chinese. However, Russia annexed the country by the back door and exerted powerful influence. Since 1949 the area has been called the Xinjiang Uyghur Autonomous Region.

Until the collapse of the Soviet Union in 1990/91, the region bordered in the north and west on the USSR, in the south on Afghanistan, Pakistan and India, and in the east on Mongolia and Tibet. After the dissolution of the Soviet Union new border states came into existence in the west: the new, now independent states of Tajikistan and Kyrgyzstan. The capital of Xinjiang is Ürümqi, although the most important city even today is Kashgar.

Islam has a long tradition in China. Even in the early years of the Christian era China had close relationships with the Arab countries. After the founding of Islam by Muhammad these relations further intensified. The exchange of goods took place by means of sea transport and by land along the Silk Roads. The Arabian merchants introduced medicine, mathematics and astronomy to China. In the other direction, gun powder, the art of paper-making and the compass came to the West.

The first Chinese Muslims were born to mixed marriages between Arab merchants and Chinese women. Today about 25 million Chinese call themselves Muslim. They are mainly to be found among the Hui, Uyghurs, Uzbeks, Tajiks, Kyrgyz and Kazakhs. The largest population of Chinese Muslims lives in north-west China, in Xinjiang, where we are at the moment. They mostly live concentrated in their own neighbourhoods. Chinese Muslims have a glorious history: they produced many outstanding statesmen, scholars, poets, doctors and scientists.

In Northern India and here in this mountainous world great world religions like Hinduism and Buddhism emerged. From here they spread along the Silk Roads over the whole of Asia as far as Japan.

---

51 previously Sinkiang, in correct Mandarin Hsin Chiang

The mountain ranges of the Himalayas, Karakoram and Hindu Kush form a great geographical barrier that divides Asia, separating the south from the north: the fertile regions of South-East Asia from the steppes and deserts of the north. For many centuries the fate of many people and peoples has been decided in this area. Central Asia was an important part of Russia's political sphere of influence. Until almost the end of the 19th century the Chinese were largely perceived as conquerors and the Russians as defenders of the strongly Islamic population. The Turkmen peoples were oppressed by China. It is, therefore, not surprising that the main aim of Muhammad Yaqub Beg,[52] who proclaimed himself Khan of Kashgar in 1867, was complete independence from the Chinese central government. His project failed. How he died is uncertain, suggestions ranging from murder by poisoning to suicide. His sons suffered a terrible fate. Some of them were beheaded, those who were allowed to live were castrated and had to spend the rest of their lives as eunuchs in the service of the Chinese.

Although China has had a policy of religious freedom on paper since 1949, the Muslims in Xinjiang feel themselves excluded and severely oppressed by the settlement of increasing numbers of Han Chinese from the east. In the years 1949 to 1973 the proportion of Han Chinese in Xinjiang grew from 3.7 to a massive 38 percent. By now (2016) the percentage must be even higher. This leads to regular revolts and unrest in the region, which are brutally put down by the Chinese central government.

According to Lamb[53] the border problems between India and China on the one hand and India and Pakistan on the other result from the over-hasty, unconsidered and artificial borders created by the British. The conflicts will continue.

The political disagreement between India and Pakistan over Kashmir is still raging. The conflict about the position of the border along the Line of Control (LOC) in the Himalaya region leads to constant fire-fights at an icy altitude of over 5,000 metres. When I spent a night close to the LOC in Dras – the coldest place in India, with temperatures as low as -40° Celsius – at a height of 3,230 metres on my way to Leh in Ladakh in 1985, the place briefly came under Pakistani fire.

The border disputes between China and India are also still unsolved. The border between these two major powers was never fixed with any exactitude and has already led to one war. However, since the Nathula-La Pass (4,545 metres) between Gangtok in Sikkim and the Tibetan Highlands was opened a few years ago there has been a certain degree of détente.

---

52 also spelt Yakub Bek
53 *The Sino-Indian Border in Ladakh,* 1975, pp. 12 and 116

The arguments between the minorities in Xinjiang and the Communist People's Republic recur with monotonous regularity, especially about matters of religious disagreement: religious fanaticism has recently increased massively in the region.

The situation in the whole region is – as we saw – still explosive. The roots of the conflict lie in the expansion of the two great powers, Russia and Britain, in the 19th century. Britain pushed the border of its Indian colony ever further to the north, and at the same time the Russian Tsar was subjugating ever more central Asian princedoms. By the end of the 19th century they had become more or less established. The British were trying to avoid a direct conflict with Russia as they were coming under more and more pressure in Europe from the growing power of the German Empire.

These movements of borders took place, however, without consulting the countries or princedoms concerned, let alone with their agreement. These borders were fixed arbitrarily by the two powers, Russia and Britain, without any regard for ethnic considerations.

I acquired my knowledge about the above-mentioned problems through many conversations with the orientalist Professor Hans Bräker, who unfortunately died far too young. One of his primary fields of research was Central Asia.

11. The Kashgar Oasis

We had actually wanted to stay in the old Russian Consulate, that was an annexe to the Seman Hotels, but there was a conference on there at the time. We'd hardly arrived when fuss and bother arose again, because Horst was not satisfied with the room they offered us. He said it was too dark – which it was. "But we can put lights on, and that will work!" was what they said to us. Oh dear, they had never dealt with Horst, who made them show us rooms for so long that we ended up with the best room in the whole Seman Hotel, with a three piece suite, a table and a bay window. After the third room I had given up going along because it was too much of an effort, and waited meekly with our small amount of luggage on a sofa in the foyer. Then Horst began to get at the Chinese woman who had taken him around, because she spoke not a word of English and every time she showed him a room that was not suitable they had to go back down to the foyer so that she could ask what the mad foreigner was on about this time. Horst complained that not to be able to speak any English was by no means acceptable in a hotel that had international guests. She should either change her job or learn English pretty quickly! At this point Horst made use of his sketchy Mandarin, which resulted in our being treated pleasantly and attentively like VIP guests by the management and all the staff of the hotel for the whole time we were there.

Now that we could finally move into our room, all we wanted was to take a shower. On the way to our room the Japanese man, who had been on the bus with us, complained loudly to the chambermaid that there was no hot water. He's got nothing to worry about, we thought, after that journey we'd be satisfied with glacier water or anything – the main thing was to get the itchy sand off our skin in any way possible. Our pride didn't last very long, because not only was there no hot water: there was no water at all in the whole of Kashgar! And we had sand everywhere; it had got through all the clothes we had on in layers: windcheater jackets, sweatshirts, pullovers, T-shirts and vests, right down to the skin, where it formed a prickly, itchy film – not to mention our hair, which was standing up on our heads, all sticky and grey. But there was no point moaning: we just dealt with the worst with our wet-wipes and wiped our hands and faces roughly clean with them. Since Sust the wet wipes had been our only way of keeping clean, because the sanitation in Tashkurgan prevented any great effort at washing.

At least here it was so warm that we could run around in T-shirt and jeans. That at least made us feel a little better.

Ill. 88: The Seman Hotel …

Ill. 89: … with the former Russian Consulate

Then we set out to find some nourishment for our tired and hungry bodies. After all, since Sust we had not only not washed properly, but we had between us only 200 grams of Tuc biscuits, and we hadn't even finished those.

Diagonally opposite the Seman Hotel we found the Café Oasis Limmin Restaurant. We knew the name from the guide book, where apart from the most beautiful restaurant proprietress on the whole Silk Road, the food also came in for praise. Since the author of the guide book had seen her, the proprietress had probably aged by thirty years, but she still looked good and the food was simply a dream. We were not able to sit in an outdoor street café as Horst had promised me on the journey to Kashgar to cheer me up. I hadn't believed him anyway: a street café in Kashgar – with the best will in the world, I couldn't imagine it. But in the Café Oasis Limmin Restaurant you could at least probably sit outside. And there was coffee too. It was just that because the sandstorm had covered Kashgar too in thick clouds of dust and a strong wind was still blowing outside, we had, on that day at least, to sit inside at a wobbly table on wobbly chairs among bicycles, lots of crates of empty bottles, a sideboard with all the crockery they possessed, and a television in front of which the whole family was sitting. The members of the family were loudly slurping vegetable noodle soup straight out of the soup dish. We were given the same soup, and to eat it they gave us an extra set of chopsticks, but no spoons. With it we drank a lot of beer to moisten our insides again and to wash the sand down. We were perfectly satisfied.

During our stay in Kashgar we more or less moved into the Café Oasis Limmin Restaurant. The outdoor tables became our living room. We ate there exclusively and drank gallons of the excellent beer. That was where we wrote all our letters, cards and also our diaries. We had seen a few restaurants that looked very good, but the problem was that you cannot get by in Kashgar with English. Even though the loveliest landlady on the Silk Road also spoke no English, she did at least have a menu listing all the dishes available in English as well as Chinese. You could point at what you wanted and be relatively sure that you would get what you wanted to eat. So for the next week we slept in the Seman Hotel and lived in the Café Oasis Limmin Restaurant.

When we returned to the Seman Hotel after our first dinner, our happiness was complete: there was water again. For me, it was too late to wash my hair as I did not want to go to bed with wet hair, as a result of which I had sand in the bed until the day we left. The shower – with hot water! – was glorious. The fact that the water leaked out from the bottom of the bathtub so that

Ill. 90:
Outside the Café Oasis Limmin Restaurant

Ill. 91:
Gazing in amazement at the foreigners

the bathroom was under water didn't bother us a bit. The main thing was that we had water. I would really have liked to start washing all our things that very evening, but we were too tired. Fortunately, all our things in the holdalls had been wrapped in plastic bags and thus saved from the sand, so that the next day at least we had something sand-free to put on.

The big wash started the next morning: we rinsed everything up to seven times, and there was still sand coming out. And from us ourselves: our throats were raw and with every sniff sand poured out of our noses. Even our holdalls had to be washed inside and out. The only washing we out-sourced was our jeans and a couple of T-shirts: the lovely landlady at our restaurant undertook to do that for a couple of cents. All the rest, the rain-jackets, thick fleece shirts, pullovers, sarongs and so on we gradually managed to wash ourselves.

After the first round of washing we went out to breakfast. Now we could sit outside at the Café Oasis Limmin Restaurant, because it was gloriously sunny and the sandstorm and the dust were things of the past. After breakfast we took a little walk in the close neighbourhood, apart from which we enjoyed a peaceful day of rest with short breaks in our restaurant. We weren't totally idle, however, since we had to bring our travel reports up to date, something for which the street café was ideal. It was not until the evening that we took a longer stroll, coming across a corner of Kashgar, which seemed to be where half the inhabitants came to eat in the evening. Pavement cafés everywhere, mostly full, and very nice pubs of the kind that you do not find near the Seman Hotel, masses of street bakeries and spice sellers. There was even a patissier with lovely brightly coloured cream gateaux and over-sweet tartlets – some even with green icing!

On our walk we also met the Englishwoman who had travelled with us on the bus from Tashkurgan. There's something strange about her. On the bus we had asked her where she was going to stay in Kashgar, and she just replied with a question: where did we intend to stay? When we answered, "In the Seman Hotel", she just said that she was going to stay somewhere else. But she didn't say where. Now we met her in the company of another young white woman, who, like her, was quite tarted up. It was obvious that she didn't find this encounter with us at all pleasant, since she just greeted us briefly and then got away as quickly as she could. It somehow seemed to me that she might be working in the horizontal profession in Kashgar. Oh well, it's my little weakness, assigning a story to everyone. We can then find amusement in the world and in other people. She had arrived in Tashkurgan with almost no luggage and, dressed up to the nines as she was, she certainly didn't give the impression of being a normal tourist.

Ill. 92: Street bakery

Ill. 93: Spice seller

The Kashgar oasis is at an altitude of about 1,600 metres and for the last 2,000 years has been very strategically important as a junction of the Silk Roads that are so important for trade. In the first century A.D. the Han Chinese came to Kashgar as they were building the Great Wall and controlled it well into the 3rd century. In the next period, which lasted until the 7th century, Kashgar was under the dominion of the Huns, which led to a long era of instability and decline. Then it returned to Chinese rule under the Tang dynasty. In 752 the Arabs conquered the region. They inflicted a crushing defeat on the Chinese at the battle of Talas. Islam subsequently became the predominant religion of the region and remains so today in the Autonomous Region of Xinjiang.

On his return journey to Venice Marco Polo visited Kashgar and described it in his travel journal. In 1219 Genghis Khan conquered Kashgar. Mongol rule under Genghis and his successors brought a golden age of stability to the whole empire. Trade flourished. The period of Mongol rule lasted until the 14th century when Kashgar was taken by Tamburlaine the Great.[54] His power extended in the 1390s from Iraq through Iran, Azerbaijan, Uzbekistan, Armenia, Georgia and Syria as far as Turkey. His death in 1405 led to a new period of instability which lasted about 350 years.

In the mid-eighteenth century Kashgar fell under Chinese control once more, under the Manchu hegemony of the Qing dynasty, until about 100 years later in 1865, Yaqub Beg crossed the Pamir mountains and brought Kashgar under his control. He declared Kashgar independent. In 1857 one of the first Europeans to reach Kashgar was Adolf Schlagintweit, a German. He was tortured and beheaded in Kashgar.

Adolf Schlagintweit, born in Munich, was a researcher, surveyor, scientist and explorer, who made a name for himself as a geologist and botanist in the middle of the 19th century, especially for his work in exploring Central Asia. Through the intercession of his friend Alexander von Humboldt he was commissioned by the British East India Company to survey the then unexplored mountain ranges in northern India and the Himalaya region. In the British press there were at first vigorous protests and objections at the choice of a German for this task, but the plan went ahead nevertheless. He sailed from Southampton with two of his brothers in 1854.

His brothers Robert and Hermann, the latter also a geographer, and he explored the area. Sometimes they travelled together, sometimes separately. But they met every few months. Adolf was the best-known of the brothers: the water co-

---
54 historically known as Tamerlan or Timur Lenk

lours he painted of Nanga Parbat are the earliest images of that mountain massif. They are regarded as masterpieces and are used by modern glaciologists as a source of comparison for measuring the degree to which the glaciers have melted.

Robert and Hermann returned to Germany early. Hermann rode from Rawalpindi in India via Nepal to take ship in Calcutta. Robert took a large number of chests containing rock samples, ethnographic objects, plants and seeds, tree sections and their entire research material including magnetic and meteorological data, manuscripts and landscape sketches, including panoramas which were up to 4 metres long, on a caravan of horses and camels to the port of Bombay, where it was shipped to Germany. In June 1857 the two brothers met up again in Berlin.

Adolf Schlagintweit wished to ride back to Germany overland via Turkestan, Tashkent and Russia. Since this route through Turkestan, at that time politically unstable, was fraught with dangers, he disguised himself as a native. After crossing the Khunjerab Pass he was captured near Yarkand and taken to the tribal leader, the Emir of Kashgar, Wali Khan. He was from Russian Turkestan and was a fanatical Muslim. He hated everything foreign. More than anything else he fought against everything that was Christian or English.

In Schlagintweit's baggage they of course found drawings, sketches of rivers, mountains and settlements. This was enough proof for Wali Khan: he was sure that what he had here was an English spy. On the 26th of August 1857 Adolf Schlagintweit was beheaded in Kashgar at the age of only 28. He was, of course, aware how dangerous his journey through Wali Khan's territory would be and had left the major collection of his drawings behind in Gilgit, so that they were preserved for posterity.

Was Adolf Schlagintweit the first victim of the fairy and nature goddess Peri, who according to legend lives in an ice palace on the summit of Nanga Parbat? The Hunzakuts believe even today that Peri protects herself against intrusion into her realm by climbers and explorers with avalanches, severe storms and snow. But she also seeks other ways to protect herself. The Hunzakuts are still afraid of Peri!

It is true that there have been many tragedies and failures on Nanga Parbat. Dozens of climbers have lost their lives on the "Bane of the Germans". The Hunzakuts are still certain that Adolf Schlagintweit was the first victim whom the fairy Peri summoned to her – not on the mountain itself, but still on what was at the time Hunza territory. He was the first European to discover, survey and paint water colours of Nanga Parbat, the Naked Mountain.

In Germany, Adolf Schlagintweit's brothers examined the scientific material that had been collected during their 30,000 kilometres of research travel in

Asia. It is still the most important collection of research material after that of Humboldt. The era of universal scholars like Humboldt unfortunately came to an end with Adolf Schlagintweit.[55]

In 2015 an exhibition "Over the Himalayas: the expeditions of the Schlagintweit brothers to India and Central Asia, 1854-1858" opened in Munich. In connection with the exhibition several hundred of Adolf Schlagintweit's water colours[56] *were displayed. The exhibition was accompanied by lectures and films and a book with the same title was published.*

After Adolf Schlagintweit's execution in Kashgar in August 1857, exploring the unknown regions in the north of British India became too dangerous for Europeans – also because of the major Indian uprising of the time. Because of their outward appearance and the language difficulties it was temporarily impossible for Western explorers to penetrate into these regions.

British colonial administrator Robert Montgomery (1809-1887) therefore organised the training of native personnel as surveyors. Known as 'pundits', they were disguised as merchants or pilgrims and sent to the unexplored regions. From 1861 they travelled the Hunza Valley as far as Yarkand. Only a few of the names of these native explorers, who performed such sterling work for their colonial masters, have been preserved.

Another European who reached Kashgar in 1868 was the adventurer Robert Shaw, who fortunately did not suffer the same fate as Adolf Schlagintweit. In the time that followed, Kashgar, exactly like Hunza, became one of the focal points of interest in the Great Game between the colonial expansion policies of Russia and Britain. In 1877 the Chinese Qing army put down Yaqub Beg's rebellion and allowed Russia to set up a Consulate in Kashgar in 1882. The British, who had collaborated with Yaqub Beg, were not allowed consular representation in Kashgar until some years later. After the

---

55 The grandson of another of Adolf Schlagintweits brothers, the German diplomat Reinhard Schlagintweit, was legation councillor at the German Embassy in Kabul from 1958-1961 and Deputy to the German Ambassador in Bangkok from 1963-1967. It was in Bangkok that Annette's father met him. After that Schlagintweit was head of the Cultural Section of the Foreign Ministry in Bonn, where Annette got to know him personally. From 1976 to 1979 Schlagintweit was German Ambassador in Saudi Arabia. I contacted him by telephone in September 2016, because on the Internet there are many suggestions that he had also been in Indonesia for the Foreign Office. The telephone call revealed that this information was false.
56 The water colours are held in the State Geographical Collection in Munich.

Manchu rule of the Qing was overthrown in 1905 and China became a republic, Kashgar entered a new period of political turbulence and disturbance. It fell by turns under Russian, Bolshevik and Dungan[57] rule, as well as that of the native war hero Sheng Shitsai. The final line was drawn by Mao Zedong when he incorporated it into the People's Republic of China. In the course of the modernisation that followed, the major part of the old city centre as well as the more than 500-year-old city walls were torn down. The People's Republic transformed Kashgar into a typical Chinese town with boring, prefabricated concrete buildings unrivalled for their ugliness. In the years that followed there are reports of frequent uprisings by the Uyghurs, who form the majority population group in Kashgar. In addition to them, there are minorities like Uzbeks, Tajiks, Kyrgyz, Kazakhs and an ever-increasing number of Han Chinese.

The Uyghurs are still fighting for their right to self-determination even though Beijing is settling ever more Han Chinese in the Kashgar region to break the power of the minorities. The official language is Mandarin, but the language most used in the Bazaar is Uyghur.

Nine years before our trip, in 1989, the Seman Hotel was ranked eighth of the ten best tourist hotels in the world. Since then things have changed a lot, because the hotel is a lot the worse for wear! But it is still the only reasonably acceptable hotel in Kashgar, and the only one furnished in the Uyghur style. Today (2016) there are many new, modern hotels in Kashgar.

In the rear courtyard of the Seman Hotel stands the old masonry of the former Russian Consulate, gloomy little buildings decorated with plasterwork and dark painted wooden floors. The old atmosphere and tension of the Great Game still reign here. Within these old buildings the hotel now has four double rooms and two suites. To spend the night in the building gives you the feeling of being in a museum. We spent hours wandering through all the rooms and the garden. Not a single member of the hotel staff was to be seen: the only company in the garden was a beautiful golden-yellow hoopoe with its tall crown of feathers and lovely black and white patterned wings.

Between the Russian-Persian Treaty in 1813 and the agreement between Britain and Russia in 1907, Kashgar was the centre of the power struggle between the two great powers, which the British, with typical understatement, called the Great Game. Both powers were aiming for economic and political hegemony in Central Asia. Great Britain wanted to have friendly nations as a buffer between

---

57 Chinese Muslims

her colony in India and Russia. After the Russian Tsar annexed one khanate[58] after another – Samarkand, Tashkent, Khiva, Bukhara, the Merv oasis and others – to his sphere of influence, the British began increasingly to fear that he was preparing to invade India from the north: Russia had long wanted to have access to the Indian Ocean. Great Britain attempted to mobilise China on its side against Russia. The Chinese began to rearm and bought great quantities of the most modern weaponry from Germany.[59]

After Germany, because of the construction of the Baghdad Railway, became a new rival in the Great Game, Britain and Russia, who had until then been bitter rivals, abandoned their competition in 1907 and directed their attention towards Germany. Among other things, this eventually led to the First World War. The Great Game of those days was of course far more multifarious and complicated than we have space for here. It was a cat and mouse game between the two great powers with the Pamirs and the Hindu Kush – not at the time fully surveyed and divided up – as the prize.

After the Second World War there was a new round of the Great Game as some of the Western powers under the leadership of the USA with Great Britain, and also Russia, tried to extend their sphere of influence in the region, especially in Afghanistan and Iraq, by military means.

So, after this short overview of the history of Kashgar and the Great Game, on with our travel journal:

The next morning after breakfast we set off to explore Kashgar a little more closely. I was dead set on riding in one of the horse-drawn carts I had liked so much the day before, as they rattled past the Café Oasis Limmin Restaurant. What I had not realised is that they are no longer allowed to travel everywhere in Kashgar. We began negotiations with one of the cart owners. More and more locals got drawn into the conversation – each of them understanding a different word.

To find someone, who could produce a complete English sentence, was very difficult, and when you did succeed in finding someone, it usually turned out that the one sentence they knew was of no use in this particular situation. Even in the hotel it was sometimes – as I've already mentioned – quite difficult. Finally! With hands and feet and a smattering of English, Turkish and Chinese we managed to persuade the cart driver to take us over the uneven cobbled streets to somewhere close to the Idkah Mosque.

---

58 Principate
59 Alex Marshall: *The Russian General Staff and Asia, 1860-1917*, pp. 79ff

Ill. 94: Travelling in the horse drawn cart

Ill. 95: Men outside the Idkah Mosque

The Idkah Mosque in Kashgar was built in the 15th century. It is the biggest mosque in the People's Republic and the most important holy place for the Muslims of China.

We were actually getting on a lot better using our knowledge of languages: we both speak English and some broken Turkish, Annette because she had studied Old Turkish and I because I had spent a long period in Turkey as an exchange student. I also had a few phrases of Mandarin because of stays in Singapore, Hong Kong and China. For preference we now used Turkish since it was almost impossible to make ourselves understood in English.

The trip in the horse-drawn cart was lovely: it went through a purely residential area that was well worth seeing. But my back did not enjoy the experience, because the roads the cart took were extremely bumpy and the cart itself had no springs. Unfortunately I had forgotten to put on my back support bandage, which I had worn for the whole trip to Kashgar. We had to walk a little way from the point where the carriage driver dropped us to the mosque, which I didn't find all that impressive, and then sauntered through the bazaar for hours, photographing 'artistic subjects' the whole time: spice sellers, bakeries, vegetable sellers, tinkers, carpenters, smiths and so on. We felt as if we'd been transported back to the middle ages.

During the whole five hours that we walked we didn't see a single tourist, which of course raised our spirits tremendously. But it wasn't just the absence of other tourists, but Kashgar itself that pleased us: the life in the streets and bazaars, the friendliness of the people and the inquisitiveness of the children were great fun. We've decided to stay a day longer than planned. The warmth here is also very pleasant after the cold of the mountains.

By the way, you can tell that the Sunday market is approaching: until now we were the only Westerners here, but now – on Saturday – groups of tourists are arriving. They are being carted in just for the Sunday market and will then travel off somewhere else on Monday morning at the latest. Today two buses from 'Exodus Overland Expeditions' have arrived. They park in the Seman Hotel's car park. The buses are open-topped and their style of travel is a kind of boy-scout tourism: the people in the group are all young and a kind of herd instinct reigns – they do everything together. They're accompanied by a Chinese guide, who looks like Horst's former boy in Jakarta, and a female Chinese guide, who constantly eats ice-lollies. As individual travellers, we of course think ourselves far superior to them and act as if we don't even know they're there.

Ill. 96: You couldn't just walk past the smell of the fresh baking

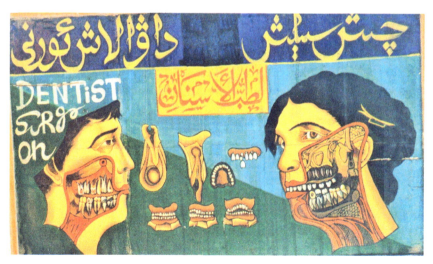

Ill. 97: Fortunately we didn't need a dentist

The national sport here is billiards. There are billiard tables at the roadside everywhere, and it's unusual to see a table where there is no one playing. And then of course there is the coming generation of billiard players, who can hardly see over the edge of the table and scrabble awkwardly about on the table with the cue, trying to make contact with any ball at all. The little kids concentrate as hard as the grown-ups when they stand on tip-toe and try and move the balls. The first afternoon we could hardly take our eyes off them because these little pipsqueaks were so funny. The majority of them aren't even potty trained, as you could see from the way their little bottoms poked out of the flaps in their trousers.

Apart from billiards, there is one other leisure activity that enjoys universal popularity among the youth of Kashgar: KARAOKE! When you stroll through the streets in the evening you can see young ladies or gentlemen in front of or inside the karaoke bars with a microphone in their hands, singing at the top of their voices! At first we hadn't recognised the karaoke bars for what they were, because there was often just a television in front of or inside the bar with a couple of chairs in front of it. It took a while to realise that they weren't showing TV programmes, but that would-be artistes were strutting their stuff. It didn't seem to us to be a particularly sociable activity, as the bold singers, both boys and girls were often sitting there alone as they tortured their vocal cords!

It's really wonderful for me to be back in Central Asia. In Bukhara, Chiva and Samarkand there are admittedly far more historical buildings, which here were the victims of Mao Zedong's cultural revolution between 1966 and 1976. But the oriental atmosphere, which makes me feel as if I've been carried off into one of the fairy tales of the 1001 nights, has survived the cultural revolution. One striking thing here is that you never hear the sound of the muezzin. Perhaps they are not allowed to use a loudspeaker for the call to prayer – or is the muezzin itself forbidden in this land of real socialism? As compensation for the loss it is impossible to avoid, from 6 a.m., the Chinese early morning exercise programme broadcast on every loudspeaker. It really gets on your nerves, and you even find yourself longing for the return of the muezzin.

Today is Sunday May the 17th. So we obviously had to go to the Kashgar Sunday market, which is famous throughout Central Asia. Until the beginning of this century Kashgar was, because of its position, an important entrepôt for the caravan trade, but even today the Sunday market is the largest market in western China, though one seldom sees camels at the market these days. Merchants and farmers come from near and far, often travelling for days to sell their goods here.

We wanted to be there as early as possible to avoid the tourists, even a few of them, that we'd seen arriving over the last two days, and so we'd set our alarm for 6 a.m. We had intended to eat breakfast at our favourite restaurant at 7 o'clock, but since we were ready by 6:30 and already on the street, we decided to breakfast after the Sunday market.

Since Horst had been clamouring for two days to have a trip in a motor cycle with a side car, we looked out for this form of transport, and were lucky. There was one standing outside the Seman Hotel, and the rider was ready to drive us to the Sunday market dirt cheap. It was a real experience. There is room for two people in the sidecar, and a third can ride pillion. With a motorbike like this you can ride through the narrowest streets where a car has no chance of passing. Horst and I really enjoyed riding in the sidecar, and the rider who took us to the market as well as the one who brought us back seemed to make it a point of bikers' honour to drive us through the most picturesque parts of the old town.

By 7 a.m. we were already at the market, and it really is an attraction. At this early hour many of the traders were still arriving with their animals and goods, unloading their vehicles and setting up their stalls. Admittedly it was no longer really dark, but the smoke that was whirled up by the vans, and the smoke from the street kitchens, which were lighting up their charcoal grills to make shashlik, produced a quite surreal atmosphere. The animal market was of course fascinating – we really felt we'd travelled back a century. Admittedly there were no camels – they apparently have not been sold on the market for years –, but there were horses, cattle, donkeys, sheep, a few goats and a couple of dogs. People were taking trial rides on the horses and checking their teeth. There was bargaining and haggling. It made a great picture and we couldn't take enough photographs.

There were fruit and vegetables in profusion. All the aromas of the Orient mingled in the air. We kept going back to the bakers, whose sesame rings gave off an irresistible odour.

Kashgar and the area around it are home to a fascinating mixture of minorities, who all come together at the market on Sundays. You get the feeling of what it must originally have been like on the old Silk Road. The Uyghur, Kyrgyz and Tajik minorities are the traders here, the Uyghurs, recognisable by their headgear, are in the majority. The Babel of languages is particularly noticeable here in

Ill. 98:
To the Sunday market by motorbike

Ill. 99:
Through narrow streets

the Pamir Knot: as well as the languages of the minorities, Persian, Turkish, Dardish, Burushaski, Chinese and Russian are spoken.

Ill. 100 and 101: Trading and haggling

Ill. 102 and 103: Vegetables and yoghourt

At the vegetable market, Horst's eyes were almost popping out of his head, even though there were sheep's offal and heads lying around among the mountains of vegetables. Fresh yoghourt was also on offer everywhere. Although it was still early in the year there were melons, grapes and mulberries, although the main crops in the Kashgar oasis are grain and cotton.

We still hadn't had any breakfast and were hungry as a result. Horst saw some red radishes, and thought he was approaching paradise. He insisted on buying some. To our question, posed by means of gestures, three fragments of Turkish and two of Chinese, the Uyghur held up five fingers and said "Beş". Horst thought that five yuan for a bunch of radishes was excessive, gave him three yuan, took a bunch of radishes and turned to go. The Uyghur, however, came after us with two more bunches of radishes. We were delighted at this example of native honesty and worked out that the five fingers had probably meant 0.5 yuan, so that for three yuan we should probably have been given six bunches of radishes. Still, we found it very fair that we had actually been given three bunches. We wandered around the market for hours: we didn't have enough eyes to take everything in. We saw hardly any tourists, and it was only as we were starting to leave that a few more arrived at the Sunday market.

It is now 1:30 p.m. local time and we're sitting in our Café Oasis Limmin Restaurant, drinking beer accompanied by salted radishes which Horst has prepared in the finest Swabian manner. What a homely delight in far-off lands! It is very hot today, 30° Celsius. Horst's eyes are still inflamed after the sandstorm, and the market also made them suffer. Fortunately I had some Bepanthen eye ointment with me and was able to treat him. As well as eye ointment, we are also treating Horst's eyes with tea-bag compresses. I read somewhere that it is soothing, and am trying it out on him. Since he's not objecting, it seems really to be helping.

After a mid-day nap we're sitting here in the restaurant again. The last few days we've been a little floppy. The constant changes of climate, the strenuous journey here, above all the heat and the dust here – not to mention our blocked noses – are all combining to make us tired. Horst's eyes are also still inflamed from the sand, but he does seem to be getting a little better. At the moment – it's now almost five o'clock – we're watching the farmers making their way home from the market with their donkey carts. With what they've bought, I hope, and not with their unsold goods. A donkey cart has just passed us with the father sitting in the front and the mother in the back, a baby on one arm and two lambs on the other. Shortly afterwards came a man pushing a barrow with three sheep standing in it. So there's always something to look at and you hardly get a chance to write.

Ill. 104 and 105: Uyghurs

Our unavoidable Uyghur teacher is just coming in to the restaurant. He explains to every foreigner – as he did to us a couple of days ago – what he is, and that he's written a book or a dictionary that no one buys. He presumably wants to sell this book to tourists, but he is so unpleasantly smarmy, that he surely doesn't ever do any business. Perhaps he just wants to get money to publish it, because I've never actually seen the book.

It's lovely watching the women here. They are dressed in the most amazing creations. Spangles, lace and frills, rhinestones on tulle in pink, light blue and orange, all of it over white underskirts. It's obviously the fashion trend of the year.

The colour combinations take some getting used to for Western eyes: for example, an orange tulle dress with green high-heeled shoes, a mauve jacket and very often a brown scarf over the head. At the same time Chinese women with the shortest miniskirts you can imagine. That's the way they go about the veil here: below often frills, lace and tulle that you can all see through, feet in high stilettos and a flimsy, brightly coloured scarf over the head. It doesn't require a Chinese woman in a miniskirt standing beside them to provide the contrast. As late as the early 20th century the women of Kashgar were famous for the laid-back way they associated with travellers.

Since 2011 Kashgar has been connected to the Chinese railway network. You can now travel by train from Kashgar via Ürümqi to Beijing. The Chinese are even planning a rail connection from Kashgar through the Khunjerab Pass to Pakistan. As far as the pass or as far as Sust might presumably be achievable. But through the narrow Hunza Valley? Impossible!

Or is it? The Chinese have also succeeded in the technical feat of building a rail connection to Lhasa high up in Tibet. At the time all the experts also said it couldn't be done. Another positive example is the KKH.

In the meantime – it's the 22nd of May – we are back in Gulmit. What sort of mental state we're in can be deduced from the conversation we've just had. Horst said to me, "Today is Ascension Day." I answered, "No, that was yesterday." Horst, "No, today is Friday." Me, "Yes, today is Friday, but not Ascension Day, that was yesterday." Horst, "But today is Friday, I'm certain about that." Me, "Yes, of course, but Ascension Day is always a Thursday." Horst, "Oh, is today Friday?" He'd got Ascension Day confused with Good Friday! I nearly died laughing. That's where we've got to after a two-day bus journey from Kashgar back to Gulmit. Still, the return journey wasn't as strenuous as the journey there: there was no sandstorm! Though it was quite eventful. But first I'll finish telling you about our last days in Kashgar.

From Sunday afternoon onwards peace returned to Kashgar. By the afternoon two bus-loads of tourists left, though not the scout troop of the Exodus Overland Expeditions. Apart from them, only two other tourist buses had arrived, which we could hardly fail to notice because such groups were obviously always put up in the Seman Hotel. What disturbed us most about the tourist groups was that they also took their meals in the Café Oasis Limmin Restaurant, which we had chosen as our living room and had until then always had entirely to ourselves. So we felt that this was a considerable invasion of our privacy. The alternative tourists of the Exodus Overland Expeditions, whose members were mainly English-speaking, lived almost exclusively on crisps, cola and beer, which was a real shame considering the excellence of the food there.

For our part, we ate our way through the menu and wallowed in delights like Vegetable Noodle Soup, or Fried Vegetable, Fried Eggplant with Tomato, Fried Potatoes with Tomato and Onion, Fried Peanuts with Tomato, Tomato Cutlet and so on. But there was one culinary delight that we did not dare attempt until almost the very end: Typical German Brat Kartoffeln! That was what it said in the menu. It seemed strange to us to order typical German fried potatoes there – almost as if we were to order pig's knuckle with sauerkraut on Bali – though funnily enough you can also get that there! But finally our curiosity won the day and we placed our order. I'm not sure what we imagined Typical German Brat Kartoffeln might be, but what we were actually served was anything but typically German. It was so good that we decided to add it to our repertoire at home – just like the Fried Peanuts we had the next day. So here are the recipes:

Typical German Brat Kartoffeln
Potatoes, raw, cut into thin slices
Spring onions, cut into one-inch lengths
Garlic, cut into fine slices
Ginger, cut into very thin slices
Soy sauce
Sauté the wafer-thin potato slices, then fry with the spring onions, garlic and ginger until cooked but still al dente. Season with salt, pepper and soy sauce.

Fried Peanuts with Tomato
Peanuts
Tomatoes, cut into cubes
Onions, cut into slices

Garlic, cut into slices
Ginger, cut into thin slices
Salt, pepper and soy sauce
Stir fry the peanuts in oil. Brown the onions, garlic and ginger in another pan, add the tomatoes and fry a little more, then season with salt, pepper and soy sauce. Add the peanuts and serve immediately.

Tomato Cutlets were just tomatoes fried in egg batter,
Fried Vegetables a pan full of vegetables fried with a lot of ginger, soy sauce and spring onions, while
Fried Eggplants were a mixture of vegetables where the main ingredient was aubergines.

We enjoyed every single dish, and we were constantly faced with the difficulty of deciding what we wanted to eat first.

The alternative tourists finally left Kashgar on Monday morning. We were glad to have the town to ourselves again for the two days until we set out on our return journey to Pakistan. All of Kashgar fell noticeably into a semi-doze. We walked around the city a lot, and particularly enjoyed the bazaar, where we bought a packet of saffron – and I bought myself a fur cap that had attracted me from the very first day. Horst also went to the barber – or rather, to two very nice female hairdressers. We discovered a lot of lovely corners of Kashgar: whole residential areas are built of mud houses several stories high, which looks very picturesque and which makes you feel you've travelled back in time, even though much of old Kashgar – as already mentioned above – fell victim to the Cultural Revolution. In these areas, however, it is possible to forget that.

On our walks through Kashgar we were constantly struck by how clean the city is: no litter or cigarette ends lying around. The area near our hotel with the cook shops and street cafés, which we had visited on our first day, is a night market. During the day, until 5 p.m., it is a clothes market. Then the clothes are packed away and the little cook shops with their tables and chairs are brought out.

12. The Return Journey to the Hunza Valley

Reluctantly, we had to begin thinking of our return journey, considering whether we shouldn't hire a car as far as Tashkurgan. Then, after all, we could stop and take a break whenever we a wanted to, including Lake Karakul, though from Tashkurgan onwards to Pakistan it was only permitted to travel by bus. Horst first enquired about private transport at the Tourist Office right next to the bus station on an occasion when he was out for a walk on his own. To his great delight he found all the staff at a German lesson, where they were learning such important things as, "Would you like to dance with me?", to which the answer was "I'm married, and I have the certificate to prove it!" But they were no help with organising our return journey.

So we asked various taxi drivers and in various pubs about private transport possibilities. In Kashgar there are a lot of VWs, Audis and Opels. We had several offers, all of which naturally cost several times as much as the bus fare, but even so we had almost decided to do it, until, at the bus station the day before we were planning to leave, we saw that the bus to Tashkurgan and then on to Sust had only been booked by six or seven people. That made us pause for thought. By the afternoon we had decided: it had to be the bus! So we rushed back to the bus station and bought two tickets for the next day. Horst also said that we should be sure that the tickets had the right date, but we both immediately forgot until we were back in the hotel. Then we discovered that the tickets had been issued for the day after next, that is, the 21st of May. So poor old Horst had to run back to the bus station to get the tickets changed. That was not so simple, as although the ticket clerk had a watch which showed the date, he didn't have a calendar. And his watch was showing the wrong date. So Horst had to go with the clerk to the nearest hotel, the Quiniwake Hotel, which fortunately was better equipped and managed to dredge up a calendar from some nook or cranny, which then convinced the clerk that his watch was making a mistake about the date. After that there was nothing standing in the way of our journey the next day and we celebrated it – as is usual here – with a beer.

There was no calendar in the Seman Hotel either, which caused problems at reception when they tried to work out how long we'd been staying there, problems which were only solved with the help of Horst's diary.

Yes, we celebrated the purchase of our bus tickets with a beer: I don't think I've ever drunk so much beer in my life as in Kashgar, but with the heat, the aridity and the dust, beer tasted better than anything else. That evening we bought two more bottles of Chinese whisky (we'd already bought one a couple of days earlier) which we intended to smuggle into Pakistan. After all, our house bar had to be restocked, as we'd used up the supplies we'd brought from Germany long ago.

The most popular beer in the People's Republic was Tsingtao, which we also liked the best. Tsingtao is a port[60] in eastern China, which from 1898 to 1919 was the capital of the 'German Protectorate of Kiautschau', which was leased from China for 99 years. The Tsingtao Brewery was founded by Germans in 1903. The original brewery building in typical German style is still standing today. Although the place name is now spelt Qingdao, Tsingtao has been retained as the name of the beer. It can be obtained in Europe, especially in Chinese restaurants. Every year there is a two-week German beer festival, like the Munich Oktoberfest, in Qingdao, which always attracts millions of visitors.

As well as Tsingtao there were also other beers of course, such as Snow Beer, Harbin Beer and China Pabst Beer. In recent years China has become the world's largest beer producer, pushing the USA and Germany down to places two and three. We were told that more and more regional breweries are being opened. We also enjoyed drinking the Löwenbräu and Paulaner brewed in China. In 2013 Paulaner was employing 15 German master brewers in China and running 16 'Brauhaus' restaurants, providing Bavarian beer and cuisine. Beers brewed in Germany and exported to China are also doing good business.

Our luggage was enriched with loads of toothbrushes and toothpaste, combs, soap, shower gel and shampoo, since although they didn't make the beds or change the linen in the Hotel Seman, they did sweep the carpet, clean the washbasin and provide two combs, two bars of soap, two toothbrushes with toothpaste and two shower gels and shampoos every day. Don't let anyone tell you that it's not a first rate hotel!

The next morning at 9 a.m. local time – this whole time thing is really nonsense, you have to keep asking which time they mean – we were at the bus station. There were rather more people who wanted to go to Tashkurgan than there had seemed to be the day before. But that's normal: it's only other people who sit in an empty bus! There were also a few Europeans whom we'd met before, and as well as them some Japanese and a couple of Uyghurs and Pakistanis. The bus was still locked at first, because customs

---

60 now spelt Qingdao

Ill. 106:
Tsingtao Beer[61]

Ill. 107:
Löwenbräu Beer

---

61 https://commons.wikimedia.org/wiki/File:Bottle_and_glas_of_Chinese_ Tsingtao_beer.jpg

and passport formalities had to be observed, but we got ourselves and our luggage into a good starting position for grabbing the best seats.

And we were lucky once again: Horst was the first to get on the bus and he immediately bagged the two front seats right and left behind the driver by spreading our bags on both seats on both sides. That stopped anyone hitting on the idea of sitting next to us. When I then got in, I was the third or fourth, we sat down and looked blankly around – our watchword was "Here we are and here we stay on our four seats," and no one dared challenge us for even one of them. We'd succeeded again! We sat on what were definitely by far the best seats on the bus, the grand balcony seats where you have an unhindered view to the front and the sides and room to stretch your legs, while the scramble for seats went on behind us. The non-local people who were travelling with us, apart from a the few Pakistanis and Uyghurs with their fat holdalls, were two Brits, an Australian with a Japanese girlfriend and daughter, a Swiss woman with an Austrian boyfriend and two other Japanese, one of whom looked almost like an Uyghur. The two Brits and the Australian with his Japanese – very primitive looking – girlfriend and her daughter and one of the other Japanese had all gone around as a group in Kashgar, where we had seen them several times since the Sunday market. The Swiss woman and the Austrian had only arrived after the market. The Uyghur-Japanese was the only one we hadn't seen before: we christened him 'gnome', not only because that's what he looked like, but also because he hopped around everywhere like a troll and – if necessary on all fours between everyone – pushed his way forward so as not to miss anything. But when his presence was needed – for example, because the bus was about to leave – you could guarantee that he couldn't be found.

Even in Kashgar we all had to go and look for him – I was afraid that the result of this major search operation would be that even more passengers would vanish. But when, after 20 minutes, he was finally found sitting on a bench in the shade enjoying life, none of the other passengers were missing. After this successful dragnet mission we were finally able to set off – an hour late, as usual.

But we hadn't got very far, perhaps 100 metres, just outside the bus station fence, when the bus driver stopped and let on another passenger, obviously a friend, who travelled to Tashkurgan without paying. It was a small, spherical Uyghur who looked like a frog; not just facially, but also because his belly protruded below the line of his belt. He got the best seat in the bus, the one next to the driver. This luxury seat was a reclining seat, and the frog, looking around with a smug expression, sat proudly down. But, oh, how could he sit there in comfort? He couldn't adjust his seat's backrest and he had to stretch his legs out horizontally. Sometimes he sat cross-legged, sometimes sideways, sometimes half in a lying position, but, however, he twisted and turned, his belly kept getting in the way. He was unable to find a comfortable position and kept sliding back and forth. But he wasn't going to let any problems show! He just kept an enthusiastic expression on his face and puffed himself up like a peacock. We watched him with barely concealed schadenfreude – after all, our seats were much more comfortable than his. Now that the frog together with his baggage had been loaded on board we could – though even later, of course – finally set off.

At first we travelled through an oasis landscape for a time, and then we were surrounded by nothing but the Takla Makan desert. Desolate![62] It must have been somewhere around here that we were stopped in the sandstorm on our way to Kashgar. For us, everything that had come after the mountains had been obscured firstly by the swirling sand and then by the sandstorm itself. After about two hours we arrived at an oasis: the mountains were already visible in the distance, although it was quite hazy that day.

In the middle of the village at the oasis our bus stopped: lunch break. That was all we needed! But since I was beginning to feel internal stirrings, I thought it might not be a bad idea to find somewhere to relieve myself. But that turned out not to be so easy. The landlord of the 'pub' where the bus driver and his smug froggy friend had installed themselves pointed us in a direction somewhere to the left around the corner and at an uncertain distance away. At first we thought the loo was behind one of the three doors that were on the outside of the building round the corner to the left, but behind the first door there was just a dead wether hanging from the ceiling, and behind the two others was in each case just a table with a couple of chairs around it: what you might call a pantry and two private rooms. And that in such a dive! So what could I do? We couldn't find a quiet corner anywhere else. Behind the building there was just a big open field with a little vegetable garden near the back wall, where a couple of tomato plants offered at least some concealment. Had the landlord offered this as a kind of public toilet?

The pressure on my bladder was getting ever stronger and the time for the bus to depart was approaching ever closer. So without further ado and with Horst's vociferous support I decided to declare the tomato patch to be the smallest room. Horst was going to keep a lookout, so nothing could go wrong. No sooner said than done. I squatted behind the plants and oh,

---

[62] No wonder the Takla Makan desert is called 'The Sea of the Dead' and the 'Desert of no Return'.

what relief. But that didn't last very long, because Horst suddenly shouted: "Someone's coming!" I quickly pulled my trousers up, but hadn't even fastened them before one of the locals was standing there, looking annoyed. It was probably the cook from the pub. Wow, was he angry and annoyed! He kept telling us, by spooning imaginary food from an imaginary plate into his mouth, that the tomatoes were meant to be eaten, while Horst loudly told him in broad Swabian that fertiliser was good for the tomatoes and that this was where we'd been sent. After a loud exchange of scurrilous expletives, which probably saved us from a good beating, we quickly left the scene, hoping that the bus would soon leave. Which, of course, it didn't, because the bus driver and his froggy friend took all the time in the world, or so it seemed to us.

We squeezed ourselves into a corner, trying to keep as much out of sight of the pub as possible, which wasn't easy, as the bus was parked directly in front of the pub. We weren't sure if the landlord's rage against us might not still be expressed physically. Horst was of the opinion that we could be glad that we hadn't been overtaken by the same fate as Adolf Schlagintweit, who had after all been beheaded in Kashgar – which was not all that far away from us. When we then saw the bus driver preparing for departure, we sprinted over to the bus, rather relieved to be able to leave the site of our – all too visible – disgrace at last. When we were safe once more we were also quite amused at this educational experience and laughed heartily!

So, in the meantime I have lightened our luggage somewhat here in Gulmit, because I have obviously, after a major washing campaign, disposed of Horst's socks down the drain. He had already washed them himself, but they didn't pass my critical inspection as sparkling clean, and so I snatched them away from him to wash with some other smalls I intended to wash even more shining white. Then I insisted that Horst dispose of the bucket of washing water for me – unfortunately with his socks still in it. But being able to lose two matching socks at the same time from a bucket of washing and not to miss them for hours is quite an achievement!

So, after this short excursus into the everyday life of a traveller, on with the journal of our return journey to the Hunza Valley. After the tomato incident in the oasis, nothing else adventurous occurred. We soon reached the mountains and were often only able to travel uphill very slowly. The bus frequently had to resort to changing down to first gear to cope with the slopes at all. I kept nagging Horst to take photographs through the bus window,

Ill. 108: Our bus

Ill. 109: Back in the mountains

becoming quite frantic when we saw yurts and camels, because I just had to have them captured on film. After a nine-hour journey – and not a minute of it was boring, because there was constantly something interesting to see – we arrived back in Tashkurgan and landed once more at the Traffic Hotel, about which we had been so scornful on the way out.

And this is where our second great deed of the day came about: all the tourists checked in, but Horst was always on the move, keeping the staff busy, asking to inspect rooms and throwing them all into confusion, while I kept an eye on the luggage. He finally chose a room, came back to the reception desk and confused the porter – who was dressed in a military style uniform – with questions, which he did not understand because he didn't speak a single word of English. Horst complained bitterly again about the fact that there was no water, which the porter did obviously understand, and tried to indicate to Horst that it would be back on soon. And suddenly Horst demanded – I could hardly believe my ears – a receipt for the room, which had not yet been paid for. The porter now began to panic, looking for the bill – which had not yet been prepared – on the floor, until Horst flushed him out with the question, "Discount?" Horst then put away his 100 Yuan[63] note with a flourish, and with the words "Later, later" turned away and stormed off with me to our room. Here Horst complained loudly that, although there was water, it was only running down the wall behind the loo and then diagonally across the bathroom, but not in the loo or the washbasin or the bath tub!

All of a sudden five workmen with one toolbox between them – though each had his own screwdriver – came into the room and began a bout of hectic activity in our bathroom. Even with five screwdrivers they couldn't stop the water running down the wall, but when they'd finished it was also running in the washbasin and the bath – and even a little in the loo.

And suddenly the porter in the police uniform was at the door and politely handed us the receipt for the as yet unpaid bill. Given this active collaboration on the part of an official of the Communist People's Republic of China we had no alternative – we decided to welsh on the bill. In view of the state of the room we regarded this as an act of courtesy, and anyway we felt that the price of 100 Yuan for staying the night on the way out was more than enough for two nights at this apology for a hotel. And in spite of the underhand way we had obtained a night's stay by false pretences we slept

---

63 At the time about 8 pounds

extremely well that night in the bed, where the linen had presumably still not been changed since the last time. Of course we spread our sarongs over it as we had done on that previous occasion. And even the gurgle of the water in the bathroom all night long could not disturb our 'sleep of the just'. As a precaution we also barricaded the door of our room before going to bed.

After an excellent – and this time peaceful – night in the run-down Traffic Hotel in Tashkurgan we were up and about early on the 22nd of May, so as not to miss the departure of our bus. We hadn't been able to ascertain the exact time the evening before, but it was supposed to be somewhere between 9 a.m. and 10 a.m. Beijing time. It ultimately turned out to be between the two, in fact at exactly 9:45 Beijing time. But this time more locals wanted to travel on the bus. Realising this, we found ourselves an excellent starting position, so that when the time came and the bus's doors opened, we just left the Pakistani, who had joined us and was having a pleasant conversation with us, standing and charged over to the bus. And, lo and behold, we had our front-row seats again! Once again we stared disinterestedly straight in front of us since far more passengers were getting on – and it actually succeeded. We had our four seats all to ourselves! However, during the journey a Japanese man asked if he could sit beside Horst, and of course we allowed this – he was no trouble.

The luggage had not been unloaded from the roof of the bus the night before, and no luggage was loaded on the roof now, so that all the luggage belonging to the new arrivals had to be stuffed into the bus. After a lot of to-ing and fro-ing all the passengers had been squeezed into the bus. The smug-looking frog had hopped back onto his reclining seat and even the Japanese gnome had got onto the bus without any delay. He had previously entered our orbit by suddenly pushing in between Horst and myself as we were deep in conversation with the Pakistani. He pointedly interrupted our conversation by asking the man we were talking to if he would get a visa at the border with Pakistan, and if it would be possible for him to travel to India overland in spite of the current disputes between India and Pakistan over the nuclear tests. And then, hop, hop, he toddled off again and disappeared for the moment! So everyone was now squeezed into the bus and we set off – for about 800 metres: we had reached the Tashkurgan passport and customs control. Everyone had to get back out of the bus with all their luggage. Now everything had to be taken down from the roof and, with bag and baggage, the assault on the customs building began. It was a real assault, because everyone was crowding and pushing in an attempt to get through the controls first – for a reason which soon became apparent to me.

They all wanted to get through first in order to be first back on the bus, because there had been another struggle to get the best seats. Foresighted as we had become, we had already lessened the risk of losing our seats by leaving – totally illegally – our jackets and sarongs in the bus. But these precautions were not actually necessary, because by now we – especially Horst – had developed a brilliant tactic: we'd put on a vacant expression and nonchalantly go to the front of any queue, and so we were more or less the first to reach the passport and customs controls and to get back to the bus.

After a lot of hustle and bustle Horst made an active contribution to the chaos by suddenly deciding that he had to change all our Chinese yuan for Pakistani rupees, which he succeeded in doing at an excellent exchange rate. But to do so he had to return to the other side of the passport control. I was afraid the whole time that the bus might leave without him! But even so he was far from being the last back on the bus. When everyone was back on the bus and the majority of the luggage had been stowed on the roof, I presumed that we could now set off. But no: another official came to check our passports. In the process he discovered that we and five others had the previous day's date as departure date in our passports! Oh no – the Chinese and their peculiar relationship with the date! But the official said that it was "No problem!" And it really was 'no problem', at least, not for the next 50 metres of our journey – because then there was another barrier and another passport check. And an official who looked as if he'd find it difficult to count up to three decided that there definitely was not 'no problem' with our passports. The formulation itself should have made us suspicious! He collected the wrongly dated passports unceremoniously with a grim look and disappeared with them. After a short while – during which we were all speculating what was going to happen, 'no problem' in China is never a good omen – he returned with our passports, no one was arrested and we now had a stamp with the correct date in our passports. And then we could really set off.

Once more we were travelling through a magnificent landscape – the weather was completely clear that day – higher and higher towards the Khunjerab Pass. The Karakoram Range was now visibly blacker, fulfilling the promise of its name.

But then the smug frog once more became the centre of our attention. Or rather: he forced himself into the centre of our sense of smell, because he now unpacked some rolls that he had acquired in the town where we had

had the break the day before – where I'd had the experience in the tomato patch. The rolls were filled with mutton which by then had seen far better days and stank abominably, which didn't put the frog off from falling on them greedily, smacking his lips. He also offered some to our stentorian bus driver – his voice was so loud we felt that he must have a wife at home who was hard of hearing –, and to our horror, he also enthusiastically dived into this stinking snack, making equally slurping noises! It made us feel really ill, and we were glad when they finally finished their meal. We were just worried that the driver might suddenly collapse with stomach cramps on the open road.

Many picturesque sights on the way – camel caravans, yurts, donkey carts – helped us to forget the mutton rolls and made the journey very rich and varied. In actual fact no more difficulties were to be expected. Now, after some of us were double-stamped, so to speak, there was only one problem that could, in our opinion, arise: the Austrian boyfriend of the Swiss woman – he turned out later to be from Liechtenstein – had been entered in the passenger lists, which the bus driver had to show everywhere, as having 'Reisepass' [German for passport] for his nationality. But to our astonishment, it caused no problems at all. All the other controls we passed through were obviously sufficiently familiar with the country of Reisepass, and so the lists always showed 1 x Australia, 3 x Japan, 2 x UK, 2 x Germany, 1 x Switzerland, 1 x Reisepass!

Even the later Pakistani controls had no difficulty with 'Reisepass' as a country, and so we finally arrived in Sust once more after a journey of 10 hours, happy though a little tired. We managed to smuggle our three bottles of Chinese whisky – 1 1/2 litres in all – into Pakistan with no fuss: no one even asked us if we had any alcohol with us. In Sust we managed to catch a minibus straight away, which brought us back here to Gulmit for a few pence.

It was like a homecoming. And now we're sitting here in the evening sun on the terrace outside our room, looking out over the Hunza Valley at the snow-capped summits of the Golden Peak, drinking Chinese whisky and feeling very good.

Horst is still thinking about the Khunjerab Pass:
Now we've crossed the Khunjerab Pass, almost 5,000 metres high, twice: once on the way from Pakistan to China and back again today. As you cross the border, which is exactly at the highest point of the pass, many things change: with your

Ill. 110: The black Karakoram Range

Ill. 111: Back in the lovely Hunza Valley again

first step from the Pakistani side to the Chinese you have to put your watch forward – would you believe it? – four whole hours. This major difference in time comes about because the whole of China only has one time zone, and the whole country lives by Beijing time, even though it is 5,000 km away. And since we were crossing the border at the westernmost corner of China the time difference was obviously greatest there. In Kashgar that constantly caused us a great deal of trouble, because, as well as the official Beijing time, they also used the unofficial local time, which was several hours different.

At the actual border at the top of the pass there is, exceptionally, no barrier. The Pakistani and Chinese border controls are each several kilometres away from the border crossing, so that the bus can cross the border between China and Pakistan at the high point of the pass without losing speed. This does, however, require a chicane-like manoeuvre across the road, since the bus driver must change from driving on the right in China to driving on the left in Pakistan. The drivers perform the manoeuvre with panache, since there is hardly any oncoming traffic here.

On the return journey from China to Pakistan we had a Chinese bus with a Chinese driver, who, presumably deliberately, did not stop at the top of the pass, in spite of many protests. He knew, of course, that all the male Pakistani passengers – as on the way to China – wished to pee on the Chinese border stone, to relieve themselves of all the frustration that had built up during their time in China. The Chinese driver, full of national pride, obviously wished to prevent this.

There are plenty of barriers on the open roads. The bus continually had to stop for our passports and visas to be checked, or we had to enter ourselves on long lists with passport numbers, profession, place of departure and destination. At least the breaks always gave us the welcome opportunity to relieve ourselves behind a rock or a mud wall.

Although the KKH on the Chinese side ran through broad valleys with well-surfaced roads, on the Pakistani side there were only narrow roads through deep gorges. In Pakistan we were able to read the road signs, because as well as the Arabic script used for Urdu most of the signs also had transliterations in Roman script as well as English translations, such as 'Dangerous Slide Area Ahead!' And when we'd once more left one of the dangerous landslide areas behind us there was always the friendly reminder, 'Relax! Slide Area Ends!' and 'Sorry for the Inconvenience!' Over the first few kilometres after the border in Pakistan we were constantly reminded to stay on the left side of the road by 'Keep Left' signs. In China we were unable to read anything as everything was in Chinese characters. It was only in the Kashgar area that we saw a few rare signs in Roman script.

Every border brings with it a loss of orientation. Everything is different: the people, the language, the customs and above all the money. In Pakistan 25 rupees were worth about 1 deutschmark, so that 100 rupees were worth about 4 DM. In China we received about 4 yuan for 1 DM, so that 100 yuan were worth about 25 DM. It's no wonder, then, that we constantly found the calculations confusing. When we were calculating price equivalents we had to be very careful. And we'd hardly got used to the yuan before we were back with the rupee again after only 10 days. Fortunately China had abandoned its FEC tourist currency, with which tourists not too long ago had to pay for hotels, transport and other things: the confusion caused by two different Chinese exchange rates would have been far too great.

You could also see an immediate difference between the telegraph systems on each side of the border. On the Pakistani side many of the telegraph poles had fallen down or been swept away by rock falls or landslides. Broken wires hung down everywhere. This system had long ago fallen into disuse. The Chinese side was totally different: here everything was in order. Most of the time the telegraph poles were on the left and right-hand sides of the road, sometimes even in triple rows. The Chinese must obviously depend on a great deal of information exchange.

The only things that weren't different were the marmots, which looked equally cute on both sides of the border; they are about 50 cm long, golden yellow in colour with black tips to their tails. Some of them were very trusting and watched with interest as our bus wound its way slowly up the pass, though some of them disappeared into their burrows immediately when we approached. We didn't know where to look first, there was so much to see. But no matter how carefully we looked on both sides of the border, we didn't see a single ibex, let alone a Marco Polo sheep.

Since our departure from the Hunza Valley only ten days have passed, but in the meantime the vegetation has changed considerably. Spring and warm weather have marched into the Hunza Valley and there has been an explosive increase in greenery.

After our return here to the Hunza Marco Polo Inn we have been promoted in rank from simple tourists – admittedly tourist with references from Mr Tonny, but still relatively ordinary tourists – to tourists of a higher order! We were met by a pile of letters, seven in all, which our host, Hussein Khan, had collected from the post office for us. That was a real delight for us! Horst had taken a shot in the dark and sent a letter from Germany to the Hunza Valley and also given my mother this address, so that even in this isolated corner of the world I was surprised to receive post. Fortunately Horst had informed our host, even before our departure, that we were expecting post. I hadn't known about this at all, until Horst asked the postmaster in the wooden shed that served as the post office if there was any 'poste restante', whereupon the latter just stared at us blankly in bewilderment. This postmaster fills all the positions from postman through letter-stamper to the head of the post office. Unfortunately, he not only spoke not a single word of English and had never heard of 'poste restante' in his life, but was also unable to read a single letter of the Roman alphabet. But our host had taken the matter in hand, and, lo and behold, our reputation in the village grew with the flood of letters. There was even the announcement of the birth of Hartmut's and Sigrid's grandson Ramon, their daughter Anita's son, and – you would hardly believe it – he was actually born on the 3rd of May, as Horst had dreamt in Dasu.

We, especially Horst, are now highly esteemed by the post official. Today Horst took a couple of letters and a package to the post office and was received with enthusiasm. The package contained specialities from the Hunza Valley to celebrate the birth of his brother's grandson, including dried apricots, apricot kernels and tumurru tea. The package arrived safe – and surprisingly quickly – in Germany.

Our post was the first 'poste restante' that had ever arrived in Gulmit. Today I again took some letters for Germany and Australia to the post office. The postmaster was clearly delighted to see me and to have some work to do. On the floor in the corner stood an old set of scales on which the letters were painstakingly weighed. Then the hunt for stamps began. Opposite the scales there was a metal box from which we took out the appropriate stamps. Now they had to be paid for. He had no change, of course. No bank has a branch on the KKH, but I managed to change 500 rupees into smaller notes, so that I could pay for the stamps at the post office. Now the universal postal official personally licked every single stamp and stuck them on the letters. I got the postmarking stamp and stamped all the letters immediately, so that the stamps would be of no use to thieves. 'Inshallah' all the letters will reach their destinations! Then the postmaster handed

Ill. 112:
The Post Office in Gulmit

Ill. 113:
The post box didn't inspire confidence, but all our mail arrived

me all the post that had arrived in Gulmit so that I could look through it, but there was nothing more for us.

We're still trying to puzzle out the mystery of Mister Tonny one and Mister Tonny two. It's lasted quite some time, but even on our first visit the question of the Mister Tonny they talk about here seemed quite confusing. Mister Tonny from Lahore with a wife and two daughters – not to mention the fact that a third daughter called Sonja has turned up in the meantime, who went on trekking tours with Khan Baig and also did some hunting. And this Khan Baig spent two months in Germany staying with Mister Tonny[64] and everything had been paid for by Mister Tonny: whisky, wine and brandy ... which seems to suggest that this Tonny was quite a toper, which certainly is not true of 'our Mister Tonny'. But finally when it came to the mention of Lahore, and more than anything the three daughters, I was certain that we weren't speaking of the same person. But they had all been so pleased to hear about their old friend Tonny that we could hardly disappoint them now. And there is still a very small possibility that it is the same Mister Tonny, whose mother, when Khan Baig, the trekking guide asked after her, I had already consigned to a place in Heaven. And this trekking guide now insists on inviting us to tea in his house. And our stinking host, Raja Hussein Khan, the great grandson of the last Mir but one, is also determined to get Mister Tonny's address and telephone number in Germany from us. But I'm sure that, no matter what the truth about Mister Tonnys one and two, our friends the Rosinys must also know Hussein Khan.

By the way, our host is of very noble ancestry and a very important person in Hunza, though his father, Raja Bahadur Khan, is even higher on the social scale. He is the grandson of the Mir deposed by the British in 1938, the one who murdered his father and imprisoned his brother because the latter was preparing to make a pact with the British against the Russians. Admittedly, in his grubby clothing Raja Bahadur Khan doesn't really look like someone of noble descent, but he is obviously a real petty prince here, and behaves accordingly. He was always respectful to us, presumably based on our friendship with Mister Tonny.

That's how the names are around here: everyone has a Shah, Khan or Baig after or before his name, whether it is our host Abdullah Baig in Gilgit, or Shah Khan, the proprietor of the Silk Route Hotel: he is endowed with both

---

64 Though someone from the area did also stay with Mr and Mrs Tonny Rosiny for a longish time.

a Shah and a Khan. We don't really know if this signifies membership of a clan, but we think it's quite likely.[65]

Oh, and something else: as the eldest son of a minor ruler, Raja Hussein Khan has already proved that he can get people to do things for him. He got us to produce a German prospectus for his hotel and type it out on a rackety old typewriter. He achieved that, even though, while we're sitting and writing in the garden, he snaffles all the biscuits we've bought in the village shop. So we are living proof that the Germans are always subservient to authority.

Ill. 114: A hotel prospectus is created

But I will not deprive you of the chance to see what our painstaking efforts produced:

---

65 Khan was originally the title given to rulers in the time of the horse-riding nomads of Central Asia. Today Khan is only an honorific courtesy title, just like Shah, which was previously only given to people connected with the royal house.

Information from the General Manager of the Marco Polo Inn, Mr Raja Hussein Khan, to our German-speaking guests:

I would like to welcome you warmly to Gulmit and the Marco Polo Inn and wish you a pleasant stay.

Our Hotel and Restaurant were built in the traditional Hunza style by Raja Bahadur Khan, Grandson of Mir Mohammed Nozeem Khan, who ruled Hunza from 1892 until he was deposed by the British in 1938. From the Hotel there is a wonderful view of the breathtaking mountain scenery that surrounds us. We make every effort to provide you with pleasant, clean rooms with hot running water and also to do anything else necessary for your comfort. In the Restaurant our Chef will prepare European, Pakistani or typical Hunza dishes for you.

Gulmit lies in the middle of the Hunza Valley. It is 120 km from Gilgit (3 hours by car), and also 120 km from the Chinese border at the Khunjerab Pass. It is only 30 km from Sust, the highest settlement in the Hunza Valley and from the capital, Karimabad.

Some information about the town of Gulmit. It was the winter residence of the last ruling Mir of the entire Hunza Valley, Mir Mohammed Jamal Khan. In the beautiful ancient centre of Gulmit you will find the Mir's Palace, the old Mosque, and a building almost 500 years old, which now houses a training centre for young girls learning carpet-weaving. Nor should you forget the museum that is part of the hotel and the Marco Polo Craft Centre, the profits from which are devoted to the training of young girls. This is another way that the family of the proprietors of the Marco Polo Inn work to preserve the traditions of the Hunza Valley.

The area around Gulmit offers the seeker after relaxation and also the walker or experienced trekker day trips or tours of several days. It is only 7 km to the beautiful Lake Borith, and the Gulmit Glacier, the Andra Fort and the Passu Glacier are within reach of a day trip. There are two nearby suspension bridges to the other side ofthe Hunza River, one in Gulmit itself and another in Hussaini. In the village of Hussaini there is also a hot spring, used by the inhabitants, but also available to interested guests.

A few important dates:
In the first week of April the apricots start to blossom;
in the first week of May there is a festival celebrating the beginning of planting;
in the first week of July there is a kind of Harvest Festival;
On the 11th of July the Aga Khan Festival takes place and fire is lit on the mountain peaks.

The Marco Polo Hotel also offers a comprehensive Tourist Information Centre where you can arrange bookings for trips to China, jeep hire and transport to all areas of the Hunza Valley, as well as the hire of experienced trekking guides. The hotel staff are always at your disposal for any questions and wishes.

You can see that Hunza is preparing to enter the tourist age, and we have helped with it, even if we don't want to see tourism there! Our host kept us working on the leaflet for a whole afternoon, and even wanted me to type the whole thing out again on his rickety old typewriter, simply because there was a mistake that had been Tipp-Exed out. I refused, and suggested that he photocopy it, so that the lighter patch would no longer be visible.

Today, the 24th of May, we've arrived back in Karimabad. By now it has become considerably warmer and we're sitting in our T-shirts on the balcony outside our room looking out over the Hunza Valley. Wonderful! The countryside is now much greener and brighter; wild roses, irises and gorse are blooming everywhere. Yesterday evening before we left Gulmit, Raja Hussein Khan brought us some gifts for Mr and Mrs Tonny, a package smelling strongly of goat, an embroidered spectacle case for Mrs Tonny and a letter. And now it is finally clear that we are dealing with a different Mister Tonny, because the letter is addressed to Mister Tonny Shoot! We'll certainly do our best to make sure the letter reaches its destination, but whether we'll manage to get the gifts – especially the stinking package – back to Germany is open to question![66] Anyway, we're glad that our Raja, our host, didn't give us the star attraction from his souvenir shop: a hand-embroidered panel depicting Pope John Paul II, about 50 x 70 centimetres in size.

On our last day in Gulmit we took a lovely walk, for over three hours, to a village above Gulmit with the very Greek name Kamaris. I had actually strained my back badly the day before by tripping over a chair, but with the help of a bandage, tablets and Horst's supporting arm I managed it. It would have been a great pity if I had not been able to get there. It was a lovely path with a glorious panoramic view, the weather was clear and bright and the sky was deep blue and cloudless. That day the air was clear and fresh and you could see far into the distance. In Kamaris Horst walked onto the glacier and the water reservoirs that supply the whole of Gulmit, while I sat by the wayside and looked at the beautiful landscape. And of course the local children came to talk to me, which helped to shorten the wait.

In the evening we chatted to Mujeeb Rahman, the hotel boy. He's the only one here who does not stink. He'd acquired five kilograms of dried apricots for us, and we brought him a bottle of whisky from China. Mujeeb told us

---

66 Note in January 1999: We did take it all with us and sent it to Tonny Shoot's address. The package and the letter were returned "not at this address".

Ill. 115:
A walk in Gulmit

Ill. 116:
We are always accompanied by curious children

Ill. 117: Rakaposhi

a lot about the Hunzakut culture, for example, that marriages are arranged by the parents. The son asks his parents to negotiate with the parents of the girl he likes. If they agree, the wedding is set for an auspicious date. Mostly, though not always, all the weddings in a village are celebrated at the same time. The preparations for a wedding last at least four days. Three or four sheep are slaughtered, and cooked in the Hunza style, that is, only with salt. The wedding itself then lasts another two days, on which there is dancing, though men and women dance separately. Mujeeb Rahman confirmed our impression that women enjoy high status among the Hunzakuts. He spoke of women's work and responsibilities with great respect: they keep the houses clean, cook, sew and look after the children, while the men **only** bring home the money and look after the fields and the animals. Mujeeb thinks the KKH is not good for Hunza culture because it brings things into the country, including foodstuffs, that are not good for the Hunzakuts. This view was also shared by other people. Mujeeb Rahman, who also likes cooking, told us a great deal about Hunzakut recipes. Here are a few examples. The flour is freshly ground just before use:

Hunza Cookery

Dawdoo
1. dried apricots
2. whole wheat flour
3. apricot kernel oil
4. salt
5. water

Apricot soup with wheat flour pasta

Ghumaldi
1. whole wheat flour
2. milk
3. apricot kernel oil
4. onions and garlic
5. vegetables
6. Hunza cheese (it is like goat's Gouda or old Gouda)
7. salt

A kind of double chapatti made of milk and wheat flour, baked in apricot oil and filled with fresh onions, grated vegetables and hard Hunza cheese.

Buruz Berikutz
1. soft Hunza cheese
2. whole wheat flour
3. water
4. apricot kernel oil
5. spring onions and garlic
6. coriander seed
7. salt

Layers of chapatti interleaved with cheese, onions, garlic and vegetables. Drizzle with apricot oil and serve cut into eight.

Tzamik-Tse-Aaloo
1. apricot kernel oil
2. potatoes
3. water
4. onions and garlic
5. ground apricot kernels
6. salt

A dish of boiled vegetables using the above ingredients

Tzamik-Garma
1. apricot kernel oil
2. chard
3. onions and garlic
4. chopped or ground apricot kernels
5. water
6. whole wheat flour and milk

Make a vegetable dish from the above ingredients. Then make pasta from the milk and flour and stir into the vegetables.

Berikutz (Haneeze)
1. apricot kernel oil
2. onions and garlic
3. salt
4. whole wheat flour
5. water
6. butter

Onion bread that is coated with apricot kernel oil while still warm.

Those were a small selection of the recipes Mujeeb gave us. We later tried all these dishes in a simple little restaurant in Karimabad with only two tables and six chairs. As you see, they are the simplest dishes imaginable, although they are very tasty in spite of the fact that salt is the only seasoning – probably because of the freshly ground wholegrain flour.

With every meal they serve the typical Hunza Valley wholegrain flatbread, produced mainly from four types of grain: barley, millet, wheat and buckwheat.

We were surprised that they used no eggs in producing the pasta as we do in Germany, but it was explained to us that in the higher areas of Hunza there are no chickens. They cannot survive at that altitude. At 3,000 metres, as in the Hunza Valley, the percentage of oxygen in the air falls to 70 %. Without eggs and with very little salt the pasta was quite hard compared with the Swabian variety, known as Spätzle, and took some getting used to for a Swabian like me.

Ever since the first Western travellers to the Hunza Valley, people have wondered what the reason for the high life expectancy and the extraordinary health of the Hunzakuts might be. It always seemed to come back to their eating habits. Apart from the mineral-rich glacier water – called glacier milk because of its milky colour – it is thought that the dried apricots and the bitter apricot kernels, that are so popular here, must play a major role in the exceptional vitality of the

Hunzakuts. Or is child mortality – which is relatively high – another contributory factor? Given the rough winter climate and poor hygiene, only the strong survive. Or the fact that in the Hunza Valley all farming is organic? Up till now there have been no artificial fertilizers and no pesticides. Even milk has never been pasteurised. There are, of course, no refrigerators. If it was necessary to keep something cool, such as butter or milk, it was hung in a container in one of the streams or channels that flow beside the houses. Even in summer the glacier water has a temperature that is only a few degrees above zero.

In every garden, beside every house, there are apricot trees. The Hunzakuts told us that there are three dozen different types of apricot. Every time you're invited to tea, the guest will first of all be served a dish with dried apricots, walnuts, almonds and apricot kernels, and often flatbread with wholesome apricot oil as well. Many a Hunzakut meal consists simply of bread dipped in apricot oil. This region is the original home of the walnut tree and so the walnuts here are particularly good and large. As well as wholemeal bread and apricots, milk is also a daily staple, often as buttermilk.

The Swiss Ralf Bircher was inspired by the Hunzakut diet to create his world-famous Bircher-Muesli, though he never visited the Hunza Valley himself.

The Hunzakuts' summer diet differs fundamentally from their winter diet. Because scarce and precious wood has to be saved for the winter, summer meals are mostly prepared raw. They eat what the fields produce: apricots, fresh when in season and then dried, plums, apples and other fruits, melons, pumpkins, cabbage, carrots, tomatoes, chard, onions, maize and other types of grain. Walnuts, almonds and apricot kernels are served with every meal. Meat is hardly ever eaten in the summer. It is eaten in the winter, because then there is not enough fodder for the animals, which therefore have to be slaughtered.

In winter meals consist mainly of freshly ground grain, with yoghourt, butter, cheese, dried fruit and meat. Over time the animals are slaughtered and eaten. Their hard, dark wholegrain flatbread is produced in both summer and winter. As a general rule the Hunzakut eats nothing but pure and unadulterated food.

The smoke from the fireplace in the centre of the ground floor of every house represents a major problem. The Hunzakuts are unaware of the concept of a chimney, and the smoke can only escape through holes in the outer wall of the upper floor. In winter the fire hardly ever goes out, as it is needed for both cooking and heating. You are almost permanently surrounded by a cloud of smoke. The consequences are chronically inflamed eyes and respiratory problems. Tuberculosis is often the cause of early death, and infant mortality lies at 30 %.

Today we set off towards Karimabad in the early morning. We had our own private transport, the man who drives for four American geologists. They arrived in the Hunza Marco Polo Inn the evening before last and are really getting on our nerves. They are apparently here to research the movement of the glaciers, but have not brought any equipment or measuring instruments. They eat their food very noisily, just like the Pakistanis: they've never heard of table manners. But perhaps that is a punishment for us, because they always have to eat what we have ordered from the chef, and they clearly don't like it. Perhaps that's why they won't talk to us. Their driver had to go to Karimabad to fill up with fuel, and took us with him. We gave him a respectable tip, which pleased him greatly.

The journey took us past the place where we had to cross the dangerous landslide on foot on our outward journey. When I saw it, my heart sank into my boots! Over a hundred metres wide and, in one place, a steep upward slope followed by an almost vertical drop 150 metres down to the Hunza River. I can still hardly believe that we climbed over it! Now there is a section of a perilous single lane gravel track about six metres above the old road, because it has not been possible to return the road to its previous condition. In this way the new Karakoram Highway is coming more and more to resemble the hair-raising previous road.

By now, the 26th of May, we're already back in Gilgit. Suddenly time is beginning to hurtle by. In a week and a half we'll be back home. Up till now it has been a wonderful, exciting journey; so much has happened that you hardly know how to begin describing it all.

When we arrived back in Karimabad from Gulmit, we were greeted like old friends. Even some of the locals whom we were not aware of having ever met before asked us all about how we had liked China. If we'd accepted all the invitations to tea, we would presumably still be sitting there chatting away happily. The people here are really unbelievably friendly. They all greet us, mostly with a handshake. And when we went for a walk along one of the water channels yesterday, children brought us flowers. In the evening we got flatbread from the baker who has his oven at the side of the road. The oven is a simple hole in the ground with a wood fire. He wouldn't let us pay for the bread.

*Ill. 118 and 119:
Invitations to tea and wine*

In the three and a half weeks we have been travelling it has become much warmer and greener here. So we decided to get rid of our warm fleece pullovers and the sleeping bag. I'd thought that the best we could do with the pullovers was to give them away, but I was forgetting that Horst is a Swabian: he managed to sell the fleeces and the sleeping bag in short order; that is, he exchanged them for food. And the 'customers' almost came to blows, as several of them wanted the things! Our special friend Sakit Ahmed got the jackets. He's the proprietor of the Baltit Bakery,[67] the little shop where we always bought minor items and were given wine to drink. He actually wanted the sleeping bag as well, but our host at the World Roof Hotel had already talked us into giving it to him. As a consolation we then gave Sakit Ahmed a silk scarf for his mother or girlfriend, and so he gave us a kilo of dried apricots! He's a really pleasant, cheerful guy.

We didn't really like our host at the World Roof Hotel – I've now learned the name – in Karimabad. He was quite young, but always seemed uninterested and was a lazy dog. It took a long time for him to offer us the good Hunza apricot jam at breakfast. Nevertheless, the hotel was really nice and clean and there was a fantastic view.

Our bus to Gilgit left very early. When we told our host yesterday that he wouldn't have to get up for us, he was really pleased, because he'd had to get out of bed early the previous day, as there were guests leaving for Gilgit. The bus leaves Karimabad at about 5:30 a.m. This had nearly caused him a nervous breakdown – if you were to believe what he said. The fact that he had locked the gate in front of the hotel, so that in order to get out we had to climb over the – fortunately not too high – fence, was something we found less than exciting.

The transport was also a real bother – but when does everything go as you thought it would? With the help of the brother of our 'very special friend' we had booked and reserved seats in the minibus the evening before. They told us that only the first bus the next morning would be going to Gilgit: it would be at the hotel at 5:30 a.m. But at 5:15 we could already hear loud honking on the street above, and when at 5:25 we reached the road after our fence-climbing exploits, a completely different bus arrived. To avoid any risks, we paid again and set off in the other bus. What we didn't know was that the buses always drive up and down the streets a couple of times – sometimes even from one village to another – in order to pick up as many

---

67 Not the street baker who gave us bread as a gift.

passengers as possible. Suddenly we saw the bus we'd booked seats on the evening before. Horst got our bus to stop, and after a bit of palaver he even got the fare money back. The driver wanted us to stay on his bus, but since our own bus was much emptier, we weren't very keen on that. It was no use anyway, since because our bus didn't have enough passengers for Gilgit, our bus driver unloaded us and two other passengers onto another minibus, handed the fares over to the other driver, and there we were again, in another full bus! But we still got to Gilgit in relative comfort. During the journey it rained a bit, increasing the danger of landslides, of course. But on that day no mountain collapsed and it was a quite unproblematic journey. In some places you could see that avalanches of scree had been removed, and in some of them the big diggers were still at work. Frequently our bus had to drive very carefully to get safely over a stretch of – single lane, of course – track, that had been driven though a landslide. We are almost certain that in 20 years the Karakoram Highway through the Hunza Valley will probably no longer exist, or will be nothing but a gravel road like the old road to Hunza. Anything else would be a miracle.

Yesterday in Karimabad we heard of at least three landslides. They are burying stretches of the KKH much more often, since the mountains have become much more unstable because of the road building, especially the blasting. That's what the locals told us. You really need a good guardian angel not to be buried by a landslide or hit by a rock-fall. We'd expected the Karakoram Highway to be adventurous, but not that it would be quite so dangerous. The proof of that was the battered bodywork of the many crashed cars that we so often saw in the gorge below the KKH or lying in the rushing river. Still, we wouldn't have wanted to miss a second of our journey to Kashgar and back, and the nearer we came to the end of our journey, the sadder we began to feel.

When we arrived in Gilgit, we returned to our former quarters in our somewhat run-down – actually quite run-down – Hunza Inn. We were welcomed with a great deal of fuss and were immediately given our old room, although we still had to ensure that the beds were freshly made, just like the first time. The aged boy explained that they were clean, shaking the bedclothes to prove his point. But when the giant cloud of dust that resulted had settled, he was immediately ready to fetch fresh bedding. We had of course looked at other accommodation during our previous stay, and there had been some rather better places that were quite affordable, but in the Hunza Inn everyone is so friendly and always willing to do what you ask, even though things are rather chaotic here.

The proprietor, Abdullah Baig, takes no trouble at all. He's a really unique character, very interested in geology and politics – he told us a lot about geology when he took us to Karimabad on our outward journey. What he loves best is sitting in the garden, philosophising with his friends. It's just rather nice here. Yesterday one of the staff came to our room, bringing a second set of fresh bedding and towels, even though we'd already been given them five hours before!

Talking of chaotic ...! There are always problems when ordering food. As we'd already discovered during our first stay, it's a matter of chance whether you get what you ordered; though there's little point complaining. You just have to eat what you're given! There are also deficiencies where cutlery is concerned: we were once served omelettes without any cutlery at all, but to make up for it we were, on another occasion, given yoghourt with a knife and fork.

During our first stay we'd already informed Abdullah Baig that we only wanted vegetarian food. Shortly before our departure he asked us, somewhat shame-facedly, "Please tell me, what is vegetarian food?" He was quite surprised by everything we listed for him, "Yoghourt, oh really? Vegetables, oh really?" But what surprised him most were potatoes, "Potatoes, oh really?"

Now it's another new day. We're sitting in the shade in the hotel garden. The sun is still shining on our terrace, and it's too hot to sit out there. The change from the cooler mountain air of Gulmit and Karimabad to the heat here in Gilgit is a bit demanding, not to say exhausting. And yet we are still above 1,600 metres here. But we have time, and can take enough time for everything. It's possible that, as it was in Kashgar, we have a section of our journey behind us where everything was very tense. Now it's over, the tension is over and we can just relax.

Yesterday we booked a flight to Islamabad for the day after tomorrow. From there we intend to fly direct to Lahore. You can't book through to Lahore from here, because they never know if the plane from Gilgit will be able to fly on the date planned. You always have to change planes in Islamabad if you wish to fly further. Departures from Gilgit depend on the weather since the pilot can only fly by VFR[68] from here. Yesterday no flight traffic was possible, but today everything has returned to normal. Because of the cancelled flights the waiting list is getting ever longer. There are three flights daily to Islamabad and there are only two seats on each for tourists; the remaining places are reserved for the military and the local population.

---

68 VFR = Visual Flight Rules, which apply when the pilot is permitted to fly using only what s/he can see

Our host has just been sitting with us, chatting. He told us about a famous polo player who was still playing at the age of 105, in a team with his two sons, who themselves cannot have been much younger than 70 or 80. The father then died at the age of 130, not because of illness, but because his time had run out. But today people don't live that long, because of new eating habits: white flour, sugar, which was previously unknown, more spices, much more meat and the fact that the animals have been injected against diseases. As a result there were new diseases, like heart diseases. There had been a decrease in diseases which had always existed in the Hunza Valley, such as problems with eyes and teeth, which did not, however, affect longevity.

Then he returned to the starting point of our conversation, the game of polo. He challenged us to bring a German polo team to Gilgit for a friendly match. The horses would be provided here in Gilgit! That would be the only way to do it: I'd like to see a polo team trying to get its horses into a Fokker Friendship aircraft! He had no interest at all in English polo teams in spite of the fact that England is the leading nation in Europe where polo is concerned. Much the same as his attitude to our visiting the British cemetery three and a half weeks before, "You don't have to see that, they have been very cruel to us!" was his comment, and so we didn't get to see the cemetery.

In Karimabad there were slogans sprayed in red paint on a wall, 'Hunza is peaceful land. Don't let USA terrorist here' and 'Don't allow American cheaters in Hunza. We hate USA!' These were the only graffiti of the kind that we saw, although the British and Americans are obviously not very popular here. Why the USA? As far as I know, they have never had a role to play here. On the other hand, they are very German-friendly – which we quite like!

Hunza is exceptionally clean. There is no litter lying around, and there are waste bins everywhere with signs saying, 'Keep Hunza clean'. Here in Gilgit it's a bit dirtier, but the people are just as friendly. Yesterday we moved from one tea invitation to another. First in a tea shop, where the proprietor – to our amazement – asked us how our trip to China had gone. It turned out that he knew us from Karimabad. On the previous evening we had been drinking tea with his cousin in Karimabad. And so we had to drink tea with him too, of course, and thus have become more or less members of the family. That's the bush telegraph in action!

From there we went to Mohammed's Book Stall to give the proprietor the Rosinys' regards. It was immediately obvious that both we and the shop owner were talking about the same Mister Tonny and Mrs Hanne! I also had the impression that the wrong Mister Tonny didn't actually waste his time in bookshops; he preferred hunting, taking a large dram with every 'View Halloo'!

There was tea again in the bookshop too, here with milk and sugar, which I always have to make a great effort to drink. But the conversation was pleasant and interesting. It was actually the bookshop owner's father who had been the Rosinys' friend, but he had vanished without trace in 1989 on a flight from Gilgit to Islamabad; in fact, not just him, but the plane and all its crew and passengers. To this very day no trace of them has been found. His son, who had also visited the Rosinys, had as a little boy accompanied the author James Hilton on his journey to Hunza together with his father. An earlier journey to the Hunza Valley had inspired James Hilton to write his fascinating book 'Lost Horizon'.

Horst has just got up to look for a four-leaved clover in this meadow where we are sitting. And he's found one and given it to me. What is even more astonishing is that he also found a five-leaved one! And I am now sitting on them both, pressing them flat with my entire body weight.

Our host, Abdullah Baig, has just been sitting with his staff, presumably discussing life, the universe and everything! Now they've all gone into the kitchen together – it's 11:05 a.m. –, presumably looking to see what can be done to keep body and soul together. You hardly ever see anyone working here. When I wiped the table on our terrace yesterday, I obviously inspired the boy to imitate me: he wiped the tables of the two rooms next to us. But that was obviously too much effort, and his keenness for work evaporated. And why bother to go to all that effort, after all, we are the only guests here.

So that we have hot water to shower in the morning Horst first has to light a boiler in the inner courtyard. As a special favour the hotel provides the wood for the fire.

There are always lots of locals here: they sit in the garden, chat and then disappear again. Yesterday evening when the muezzin called, three of them knelt on a sheet in the garden and began to pray. We were standing one floor higher, watching them with a glass of whisky in our hands: we thought ourselves very blasphemous! After a while – the one who was leading the prayers appeared not to want to come to an end, and the other two seemed to be getting quite anxious – the prayers were finished and they disappeared out into the street. There is always something to watch here: for example, yesterday evening a very distinguished looking local was here with a companion. He also sat in the garden talking to his companion, picking his nose the whole time. He obviously managed to excavate something, which he then proceeded to smear on the edge of the table. Very appetising! And yet he looked so posh! I was bitterly disappointed; that was not how I'd expected a posh Pakistani to be.

Horst has just come back, totally delighted that the washing we did this morning is already dry! Now he's trying to work out what else we can wash. I wanted to wash the curtains, which have probably last been clean when the hotel was opened in 1978; Horst would have preferred to follow in my mother's footsteps. She lost all control in Pagan in Burma: she was so enthusiastic about the way things dried so quickly that she washed the floor mats from our room. But Horst has meanwhile unstopped the blocked loo, and that's calmed his thirst for action somewhat. I assume that he will not have time before we leave to mend the cracked loo seat which keeps biting our bums!

Today, the 28th of May, it's beginning to look as if we won't be able to fly from Gilgit tomorrow as planned. It's 4 p.m. now, and it's still raining cats and dogs – and how! We've been soaked through twice today and I fell over in the mud once on our way back from our second visit to PIA[69] today. The first time we were too early and could not be issued with tickets for tomorrow. Today all flights were cancelled because of the weather, and everyone who was booked on a flight today had to reconfirm their booking by 12 noon today, or lose their right to a seat on tomorrow's flight. There is a strict order to proceedings: if flights are cancelled on a particular day, all the passengers have the right to a seat on the next day. Those who are booked for the next day go to the back of the queue, unless some of today's passengers have failed to reconfirm their bookings, in which case their seats become available and you may get lucky and slip onto an earlier flight. So you see it can take quite some time to get out of Gilgit by air.

When we went to the PIA office the second time, Horst used his powers of persuasion and got very chummy with all the airline staff, particularly the boss, while I of course remained well-behaved and modest in the background, as was fitting. And what do you know, we got tickets for the first flight tomorrow morning. That means, the first flight to take off from Gilgit will take us, whenever that is – though we will have to reconfirm our booking every day to make sure. At the moment we are not holding out much hope for tomorrow.

---

69 **P**akistan **I**nternational **A**irline, popularly also **P**lease **I**nform **A**llah

Afterwards we had a lot of time and were able to stroll through the bazaar at our leisure. We always find markets fascinating. There were all sorts of things there: carpets from Chotan, silk of all colours, cheap linen cloth, caps, boots, radios from Japan and Russian perfume, but we returned to the hotel with nothing but a couple of kilograms of dried apricots. The dried apricots here taste so wonderful that we want to fill our pockets with them for the journey home.

The constant rain means that it has become quite cool. We've put all the things that we tore off on arrival in Gilgit back on. The pullovers we sold wouldn't be bad either, because our rain-jackets, which we put on to keep warm, were soaked in our first venture out into the rain and now need to dry. Perhaps we'll sell them off too – but only when the rain has stopped!

Since yesterday I have suffered a lot of bites – but only on my arms: fleas? Bugs? But where from? After a cockroach crept out of Horst's bed yesterday evening, I feel that anything is possible. I haven't got any insect-bite cream with me, so I've rubbed myself with aspirin solution, and hope that it will help with the itching. There are at least thirty-five bites so far, on just one arm!

Ooh, I'm shivering now! We're waxing lyrical about tiled stoves and a cup of coffee or a glass of wine and a good book to go with it. And here? Horst has just been sitting on a dead bird without realising it and he's now frightfully nauseated. We're paying thousands of marks to shiver in the rain here in Gilgit. But at least the fact that we can laugh about it helps to keep us warm inside.

It's the 29th of May and we're still in Gilgit, but no longer shivering. Today the sun shone again and the mountains all around, which were shrouded in thick mist yesterday, were covered in snow almost down to the level of the valley. But in spite of the sunny weather no flights could come from Islamabad because there was still bad weather en route. But in the sunshine and a T-shirt we can survive another day here. Our host, Abdullah Baig, cheered us up yesterday by pointing out that in every extended period of bad weather in recent years the sky looked exactly as it has done yesterday and today. The last time, no planes could fly for two weeks and the whole KKH was shut for three weeks because the constant rain caused so many landslides. Even the military with their helicopters couldn't get through to Islamabad.

As we were discussing whether in the worst case – after all, we have to catch our plane in Islamabad in a week's time – we should hire a car again or take on an 18-hour non-stop bus journey, Abdullah Baig said that a car would be very bad in the rain. It would be better to travel by bus, since it would have a thicker roof in case of rock falls. But he would advise us to avoid both options in weather like this and wait for the next flight. Oh well, in spite of all this Job's comfort the weather is better. After two hours waiting at the airport we were informed that all flights were cancelled for today, but that the chances were good for tomorrow.

But yesterday still held some surprises for us! As I've said we – especially I – were freezing and we withdrew to our room for our evening meal. There was flatbread with spreading cheese, cucumber and onions. True to the old Hunza rule for eating while travelling we each eat a raw onion every day.[70] And we enjoy our onions with cucumber, cheese and bread, because that always seems to us to be the culinary highpoint! Perhaps it also helped us to avoid even worse stomach problems. Anyway, we were sitting in our room and enjoying our food. The second Hunza rule, never to drink while eating so that you chew more thoroughly was not something we adopted.

We were drinking a whisky to crown the meal when suddenly there were loud bangs in the street. At first we thought it was fireworks, but it soon became quite clear to us that it was rifle and machine gun fire. My first reaction to Horst was, "This is all because of your bloody sneezing!" This was because in Karimabad I had made the observation, that if the hostilities between Hunza and Nagar broke out again, it could only be because of Horst's eruptive sneezing from our balcony in the direction of Nagar. Horst must be the world's number one in loud sneezing! His booming 'Atchoo' would echo three times back and forth from the high mountains. Finally, in Karimabad it became quite noticeable that every time Horst sneezed towards Nagar the muezzin would start up loudly in response.

At any rate, the gunfire around the hotel was getting heavier and heavier and Horst went out to see what was actually happening. One of the staff ran through the garden with a rifle, another hid behind the corner of the building, and the proprietor sent Horst straight back to our room. Suddenly everything went dark. A power cut! We'd put the light out anyway, in order to be able to see better what was going on outside. We still did not know what was happening, and the shooting grew louder and louder and spread

---

70 Note 17.2.1999: By now I know that to be correct one should eat a raw onion with every meal.

all over Gilgit, though around our hotel it began to die down. Careful as we are, we had first hidden our whisky under the bed in case it was conflict between Shiites and Sunnis so that we might find a couple of fanatical Shiites standing at our door. We were not afraid for our lives at any time, but we were concerned much more about losing our precious whisky.

The shooting had been going on for about an hour when there was a knock at our door: our host was standing there with a candle, and he explained the reason for the shooting. They were celebrating the first successful Pakistani atom bomb test, and it had been a suitable occasion to test their own weapons at home! It was necessary to be armed against India. We should still not go too far from our room in case we accidentally got shot in the dark, but there was no real danger. We immediately dragged the whisky out again and celebrated our rescue from the Shiites with a hefty draught, while listening to the news on our little short-wave radio. The German news station gave us more information about the tests and the reaction to them around the world. A state of emergency was declared this morning.

After reconfirming our flight so that we didn't lose our place in the queue, we went to see Horst's new 'friend' here in Gilgit: Mister German! In the Hunza Valley Horst had succumbed to German fever. In 1974 his brother Hartmut had stayed in Karimabad with the Mir's secretary, a Mister German, and Horst had left no stone unturned trying to find him. He got wind of all kinds of different reports: Mister German is dead, Mister German has a shop in Karimabad, Mister German has a hotel in Gilgit. He gradually discovered that there must be at least three Mister Germans in the Hunza Valley, and that German is not a local name, but just refers to the fact that the person whose name it is has some connection with Germany or Europe. Even though it soon became clear that the Mister German he was looking for was dead, Horst still didn't throw off his German fever. He was interested in the Gilgit German, because there was a story that he had fallen out of a hotel window in London and had lost an arm. And so Horst sought him out. A Hunzakut who can climb the highest mountains here like a mountain goat and yet falls out of a hotel window in London must be something special!

Mister German did in fact have two arms, but couldn't use the right one. Anyway, we were both invited there to tea, and today went back to take down the address in Cologne of some people Mister German had once lived with and wanted to be remembered to. And now I know where I got the bites. Horst too now has a large number. Fleas in the German family sofa have made a major assault on us! Horst can tell you about Mister German and his colourful history himself: he did, by the way, actually fall out of a hotel window in London when he was drunk for probably the first time in his life.

My brother Hartmut had been in Karimabad in the Hunza Valley with his son Olaf twenty years before us. It was the time shortly after the Mir had been compelled to hand the reins of government to Pakistan. At that time the journey must have been even more arduous than it is today. There were no hotels yet, and no guest houses or restaurants. Hartmut and his son had stayed with the Mir's secretary, a Mister German. Since that time a great deal has obviously changed, but the surreal, impressively beautiful landscape, the lovely green valley surrounded by threatening black mountain ranges, behind which tower snow-decked peaks with glaciers which flow down as far as the valley, is still the same. It's just wonderful – you would think you'd found James Hilton's Shangri La.

Hartmut asked us to look up Mister German and give him his regards. At the time, in 1974, visitors to the Hunza Valley were still a rarity, and his son Olaf was then the youngest foreigner ever to visit the valley. On our first visit we enquired about this Mister German, the Mir's secretary, and discovered that he was already dead. We didn't give up and asked our host at the Hunza Marco Polo Inn, Mr Raja Hussein Khan, to enquire about Mister German's family in Gulmit: it had been the Mir's winter residence, and our host still had close contact with the Mir's family.

And immediately after our return from China we were bombarded with the latest information. There are still two Germans in the Hunza Valley; one of them was an elderly merchant in Karimabad and the other lived in Gilgit and only had one arm. German wasn't a real name, they both had it because they had both been in Germany, and the second one had lost his arm after falling out of a hotel window. The Hunzakuts are actually human chamois, who learn to climb before they learn to walk. Everything here is a climb, whether on foot, on horseback or on wheels. And a Hunzakut is supposed to have fallen out of a window? The story interested me!

Back in Gilgit we had a conversation over tea with Mr Ikram E. Beg, the owner of the only bookshop in the town, the Bazaar Mohammed Bookshop. As an eight-year-old he and his father had accompanied the American author James Hilton. They had spent days walking around Hunza Valley.

I naturally also asked Ikram E. Beg about the mysterious Mr German, the Mir's secretary. He confirmed that he had died 10-15 years before. But I was seized by German fever, and asked about the other Mister German. He knew him too: he was the manager of the Mountain Refuge Guest House. So I set straight off to meet him. However, he did have two arms – it was just that the right arm was lame. I told him about Hartmut and his Mister German. He said that that was a different family. His own real name was Ibrahim Baig, but from the time of his youth he had only been known by the name German because he had always dressed in European clothing and had always been interested in German technology, engines and German cars. After visiting Germany his real name had been completely forgotten and he was only known and registered – even by the authorities – under the name of German.

Over the customary cup of tea he told us his story: in his youth he had guided visitors to Hunza, to the Swat Valley and to Chitral. At the beginning of the 1970s he had guided a German industrialist from Cologne in the area around Gulmit, and on the trip they had discovered an old 1929 Chrysler, which the German immediately bought. Mister German got the old Chrysler working again and in 1974 he drove it to Germany via Iran and Turkey. His employer, the Cologne industrialist, together with his girlfriend and a German shepherd dog, had come along for the ride. However, the two Germans were arrested en route for illegal arms possession, because they had wanted to smuggle not only an old car but also guns into Germany. While they were in prison in what was then Persia, German had to sit tight with the Chrysler and the dog, of which he was mightily afraid!

After the industrialist and his girlfriend were released, they continued their journey. The old-timer ran like a dream and they reached Germany safe and sound. The industrialist was able to exchange the old Chrysler in Germany for a Porsche. German liked Germany so much that he decided to stay for a while. He worked as a lorry driver for the man's firm in Germany until the end of 1976, all the time without a valid driver's licence! And at this point he demonstrated that he could speak quite passable German.

He stayed in Europe until 1980, in France and England, until he was seized by homesickness for Hunza. His fall out of the hotel window had, moreover, been in England and not in Germany. A gang had got German, who until then had been teetotal, drunk in London, then robbed him and pushed him out of the hotel window. This obviously rescues the Hunzakuts' reputation as vertigo-free! After the fall German spent several months in hospital, but his right arm remained paralysed.

After we returned to Germany I contacted the man in Cologne and his girlfriend – who was by now his wife. The couple confirmed that German's story was true in all its details.

Back in the Hunza Inn I wrote up the events of the previous days. When I stood up, I discovered that I'd been sitting on a dead bird, and when I went to my rucksack a cockroach jumped out at me. And Annette is complaining about 40 new fleabites, especially on her arms, while I have 25, mainly on my legs. These are lasting reminders of afternoon tea with Mister German, his delightful young wife and their little daughter Noorina. But none of that can spoil our pleasure in this journey.

Now, on the 30th of May, we're sitting in Faletti's Hotel in Lahore, thinking about the fact that I was here with my parents in October 1992 and stayed in a room only two doors away. Horst and I drank our first sundowner to my parents, a little sad, but glad that we were able to stay here one more time, because Faletti's Hotel is being sold to the Holiday Inn group, which intends to completely renovate it, so that the old colonial hotel will presumably become as unaffordable as the Strand Hotel in Rangoon. But it is absolutely necessary for it to come into private ownership because it has become terribly run-down. Our section of the hotel, where we stayed in 1992 – it's called Luxury Class –, has perfectly acceptable rooms, but you have to look very hard to find a bit of the hotel that's half-way photogenic.

We had a very educative experience as we were checking in. Horst of course tried, as always, to get the price reduced, and pointed out that we – even though he'd never been in Lahore before – had often stayed there, and that my parents had stayed there frequently since 1960. The manager, who'd been there for 27 years, immediately 'recognised' Horst, and greeted him enthusiastically – but he didn't remember me at all, even though I had actually been a guest there. And even for an 'old customer' like Horst there was only a small drop in price. A shame, but we stayed here anyway.

At the moment all Hell's been let loose outside: Pakistan carried out its sixth atom bomb test today and the populace is going wild with enthusiasm. Motor parades are driving through the streets with much hooting of horns, fireworks are being let off and there is a lot of shooting into the air. The Mall is lined with thousands of people, because it is on the route the Prime Minister, who is going to give a speech in the great Badshahi Mosque, will drive along.

But let's go back to the beginning: this morning in Gilgit we woke up at 4:30, and our first look through the window told us that there would be a good chance of an aircraft flying into Gilgit today – and then flying out again. The sky was cloudless! We'd actually set the alarm for 5:15, but by the time it went off we were almost ready for departure. The evening before we'd gone to bed very early, because we'd had to get up in the early hours of that morning – after all, we'd actually hoped to fly out yesterday. But after a lot of humming and hawing it became clear that the weather was not good enough and we'd have to stay another day in Gilgit. By 6 o'clock we were already punctually at the airport and were taken straight in to the boss, whom we knew from our previous visits. We had a long chat about God, the world and Annemarie Schimmel, whereupon he immediately told us that he would ensure that we get the best seats on the plane: VIP seats with a view of K2 and Nanga Parbat! The reason was Annemarie Schimmel, whom I knew from my university days. And the PIA boss was very helpful in other ways too.

Annemarie Schimmel was the most important German academic of her day in Islamic Studies. She died in Bonn in February 2003. She was very gifted: by the age of 15 she could speak Arabic, among other languages. She took her doctorate at the age of 19 and at the age of 20 she became the youngest ever professor of Arabic and Islamic Studies at the University of Marburg. She had doctorates in a number of subjects, as well as honorary doctorates from Turkey, Persia, India, Pakistan and Sweden among others. She published more than 100 academic articles and books, and was awarded the German book trade's Peace Prize in 1995. As well as German she spoke English, French, Swedish, Italian and the oriental languages Arabic, Persian, Turkish, Urdu, Sindhi, Punjabi, Pashtu and Kurdish. She was a linguistic genius.

Annemarie Schimmel visited Pakistan countless times, the country she regarded as her second home, and where the great orientalist is even today revered almost as a saint. She was allowed entry to all the mosques and gave talks and lectures to thousands of reverently listening people. The Pakistani government awarded her their highest civil honour, the Hilal-e-Imtiaz. Streets and squares in Pakistan are named after her, and in Lahore there is the Annemarie Schimmel House, where readings, lectures, concerts and exhibitions constantly take place.

After holding the Chair of Indo-Muslim Culture at Harvard University in the USA, she returned to Germany, to the University of Bonn. Here Annette made the acquaintance of this extraordinary woman in the course of her degree in Malay Studies and Religious Studies. Annette attended many of her lectures and was a mine of information about the life of Annemarie Schimmel. Annette was particularly taken by the study of Sufism, the mystic branch of Islam so beloved of Annemarie Schimmel.

As Annette was telling us all this, the office of the PIA manager at the airport became increasingly full. The word had got around that a former student of Annemarie Schimmel was here. Naturally no one wanted to miss this. The office was full to bursting and everyone was listening reverently to what she had to say.

To reach Gilgit, the plane has to fly through a gorge so narrow that the wingtips almost touch the rugged rock walls on either side. It was only when we heard the loud humming of the flight arriving from Islamabad that our solemn gathering could be ended, and so it was no surprise that our acquaintance with Annemarie Schimmel opened all doors and ensured us the best seats on the flight.

The people here are generally enormously friendly and helpful. Whenever you ask a question, there is always someone nearby who will help you on your way. With our flight we were among the very few fortunate people who were able to get to Islamabad today – thanks to Annemarie Schimmel! We were certainly very lucky, because the Karakoram Highway between Gilgit and Islamabad was impassable for ten kilometres because of landslides. Not a single vehicle got through by land. The extreme rain caused this, and the waiting list for potential passengers became almost endlessly long.

But we almost had to travel without our precious Chinese whisky, which I had in my hand luggage together with some fruit juice: it was discovered at the very exhaustive security check at the airport! We had to unpack the bottle, and when asked what it was, Horst answered, as if the word WHISKY wasn't clearly printed on the label, "Medicine for the stomach. When we are not feeling well, we take a little drop." The head of security wanted to test this. He had a glass brought, and when he was about to pour some out, Horst immediately interrupted him with the words, "Not too much, it is very strong". I was quite perplexed at such barefaced cheek and thought, "Now they're obviously going to confiscate the whisky, we'll have our boarding passes taken away and we'll be thrown off the flight!" But nothing of the sort happened. To preserve the honour of the Pakistani security officers, we were just politely asked to put the bottle of whisky and the fruit juice in our hold luggage, as it was prohibited to carry bottles in cabin luggage. Almost all the other passengers actually had water or fruit juice bottles in their hand luggage, but this action served to preserve the proper order and no one lost face. And so we've saved our last whisky as far as here in the Faletti's Hotel. We had deliberately been economical enough with it to be able to drink a nostalgic toast to our parents here. Perhaps it was Annemarie Schimmel who saved our whisky for us in this strictly Muslim country!

13. The First Westerners to Visit the Hunza Valley

The first Westerner to visit the Hunza Valley after the troops of Alexander the Great was almost certainly the Venetian Marco Polo. Further visitors followed in the 19th century: I've already written about the Schlagintweit brothers, of whom Adolf Schlagintweit, who travelled through the Hunza Valley in 1857 on the way from Gilgit to Kashgar, was by far the most important.

Ten years before Adolf Schlagintweit the explorer Waldemar Prinz von Hohenzollern, a friend of Alexander von Humboldt, visited the Karakoram Range and the Hindu Kush from Kashmir over a period of two years. He discovered that as yet unknown cultures survived in the princely states in those remote valleys.

After the British brought Kashmir and the Indus region under their control in 1846, the British crown sent out geographers, ethnologists and other scientists northwards to explore the areas around Gilgit. The Austrian Gottlieb Wilhelm Leitner, whom I have already mentioned in the foreword, entered the service of the British in India. In his role as a philologist he travelled the region around Gilgit and Hunza several times. In his account, published in 1856, Hunza[71] is exhaustively described. Further works followed in 1871[72] and 1889[73].

The British Colonel John Biddulph followed in his footsteps. He too was a philologist, stationed as Political Agent in Gilgit from 1877 to 1881. During this time he travelled extensively in Hunza to study the Burushaski language. His works were published in 1880[74] and 1882[75]. His home in Gilgit survives to this day and is preserved as a museum and research institute.

Another Briton, Colonel David Lockhart Robertson Lorimer, was also a philologist and was similarly stationed in Gilgit as Political Agent from 1898 to 1903. He too was interested in Hunza. At the beginning of the 20th century he published several works on the region and the Burushaski language.

The future Viceroy of India, Lord George Curzon travelled the Pamir mountains in 1894. In 1897 he wished to make the acquaintance of the King of Hunza, Mir Mohamad Nazim Tham. Lord Curzon travelled to Karimabad accompanied by Colonel Chamberlain. They were received hospitably by the Mir. It was this VIP visit that first made it clear to the Mir how great the im-

---

71 He calls the kingdom Hanza
72 *The Races and Languages of Dardistan*
73 *Hunza and Nagyar/Nagar Handbook*
74 *The Tribes of Hindu Koosh*
75 *On the Birds of Gilgit*

portance of the Hunza Valley to Great Britain and the other great powers was. Since the Mir's palace had no guest quarters as yet, Lord Curzon and Colonel Chamberlain camped in the palace garden.

During their friendly conversations the Mir learned that Lord Curzon also wanted to visit the Chitral Region, which borders on Nuristan.[76] Chitral is a high mountain valley, 1,500 metres above sea level: at the time it was hardly accessible. It is inhabited by a strict Islamic population of a few thousand. The paths were in a very poor state and even in summer the three passes into Chitral were barely passable – in winter Chitral was totally isolated from the rest of the world. The simplest access route then and now was from Jalalabad in Afghanistan. In 1947 Chitral affiliated itself to Pakistan, but was only officially integrated into the state of Pakistan in 1969. In order to create better connections between Chitral and the Indus Region work was begun in 2005 on the Lowari Tunnel, which should permit access all the year round. The building work should be completed in 2017.

Since the journey to Chitral was very arduous and dangerous, the Mir offered to accompany Lord Curzon, since he was friendly with several of the nomadic tribal chiefs along the route, an offer Lord Curzon gratefully accepted. The Mir felt himself responsible for the future Viceroy. The expedition had to be kept secret from Russia and China, because the route passed through Cossack-controlled and Chinese-occupied territory. They set off northwards accompanied by 20 Hunzakuts, the Mir of Hunza riding a shaggy yak and the future Viceroy of India likewise. Two kings on muscular, long-haired beasts – what a sight that must have been!

After seven days they reached the valley of the Khunjerab River. After crossing the 4,703 metre Mingteke Pass[77] between Hunza and Xinjiang at the eastern end of the Hindu Kush range, they then had to deal with the extremely dangerous 4,827 metre Kilik Pass (today the KKH runs south of the pass). They were now already in the Pamir Mountains. In the snow and ice region of the Kilik Pass the Mir handed Lord Curzon on to his friend, the nomad chief Qazim Beg. Having fulfilled his obligations, the Mir then returned to his palace in Karimabad. Now accompanied by Qazim Beg, Lord Curzon arrived at the Chitral Valley via Sarhad-e Wakhan. Considering that Lord Curzon had in his youth suffered a back injury in a riding accident which caused him extreme pain for the rest of his life in spite of wearing a steel corset, this difficult and extended journey was quite an achievement. Lord Curzon published travel descriptions of this region in 1896[78] und 1911[79].

---

76 Today part of Afghanistan
77 Also known as the Mintake or Mintaka Pass
78 *The Pamirs and the Source of the Oxus*
79 *On the Indian Frontier*

During the ride Lord Curzon promised the Mir that he would invite him to India when he became Viceroy in two years' time. He kept his word during his period in office from 1899 to 1905.

The next visitor to the Mir of Hunza was the British General, later Field Marshal, Lord Kitchener, who had taken over as Commander-in-Chief of the British forces in India in 1902. Like Lord Curzon he wished to secretly visit the border area of Xinjiang in the Pamir Mountains and the districts just over the border, as well as to explore the Mingteke and Kilik Passes. He too wished to ensure the support of the Mir of Hunza. Lord Kitchener regarded the Pamir Knot and the Hunza Valley as vital to British strategic interests.

The Mir assured Lord Kitchener of his support and wanted to join the mission with a number of armed Hunza warriors and mountain guides. The old Marco Polo route had become partly impassable and had to be repaired before they could proceed. They reached the Mingteke Pass via Misgar, then over the border they went back into the Hunza Valley over the Kilik Pass. The Mingteke and Kilik Passes were at the time the most important passes from the upper Hunza Valley to Xinjiang. Beyond the passes the borders in the Tarim Basin were still the subject of dispute between Hunza and China. These border disputes (by now between Pakistan and China) were not settled until 1963.

Back in Karimabad Lord Kitchener thanked the Mir profusely and there was a great banquet. The Mir of Hunza was also received by the Earl of Minto, Curzon's successor as Viceroy, and in 1911 he was even presented to King George V.

Even in the First World War the tension between Britain and Russia over the Pamir Knot did not abate. There was also the fact that the Turkmen tribes in Xinjiang sympathised with the Ottoman Empire and its ally, imperial Germany. There were constant attacks on the British and Russians and their establishments by Turkmen tribesmen.

At this time Lord Curzon was British Foreign Minister and Lord Kitchener was Minster of War. Several thousand British and Russian subjects were living in Xinjiang, and they now became reconciled in order to fight their mutual enemy, the German Empire. China remained neutral, even though the United Kingdom spread the rumour that Germany had several divisions on the march with the aim of conquering China. At the time German troops were only in the Ottoman Empire to guard building works on the Baghdad railway.

There were no German divisions in Xinjiang, but there were two Germans pretending to be Norwegian mining engineers. They were general staff officers from the German Embassy in Beijing, who were heading for Kabul in Afghanistan on a secret mission. They were crossing the desert on two ponies with a pack mule to bring support to the head of the German Mission in Kabul, Werner-Otto von Hentig[80]. They reached the Tarim Basin and were looking for the way up into a pass that would enable them to reach the Hunza Valley. The two men aroused the suspicions of the British Consul in Kashgar, George Macartney, who asked the British Political Agent in Gilgit to apprehend and arrest them.

Hermann Schäfer, the author of the book 'Hunza: Ein Volk ohne Krankheit' [The Hunza, a People without Sickness],[81] visited the Hunza Valley in 1977. While there, he had the opportunity to read the diary of the Mir of Hunza at that time. He was the first to write about this hitherto unknown case:

The Mir was asked by the British Major James on behalf of the Viceroy to arrest the two Germans and hand them over to the British Political Agent in Gilgit. The search party of troops found the two Germans wandering around in the mountains because they could not find the way up to the Mingteke Pass (at that time the most important pass into the upper Hunza Valley). In spite of their vehement protests they were arrested and taken to Passu in the Hunza Valley over the Mingteke Pass. Crossing the pass at an altitude of almost 5,000 metres turned out to be very difficult because of snow, ice and storms. The two Germans suffered serious frostbite to their hands and feet as well as severe altitude sickness. This information reached the Mir by courier before their arrival, and so when they got to Passu there was a healer waiting for them, who treated the frostbite with herbs from the alpine meadows and other salves. By the time they reached Baltit, they were already on the road to recovery.

The two officers were held in separate rooms beneath the old palace building, but treated well. The Mir was surprised that there was war between the British and the Germans: they looked similar and had the same eyes, he wrote. Under interrogation by Major James the officers – one was a lieutenant, the other a major – disclosed their secret and admitted that they had been trying to get into India by back roads. They had simply lost their way. The lieutenant was fluent in the Turkic languages of Xinjiang, and the major had perfect English: there were therefore no communication problems between the Mir and Major James and the two Germans. When their baggage was searched they found a rifle and two

---

80 Von Hentig had previously been an Attaché in Beijing, Constantinople and Teheran. In 1915 he was transferred to Kabul to foment rebellion against the British among Indian tribes and rulers. Kabul played a similar role in the Second World War (see Geerken, *Hitler's Asian Adventure*, pp. 305ff). In WW2 von Hentig was assigned to take care of the Grand Mufti of Jerusalem, Mohammed Amin al Husseini (see Geerken, *Hitler's Asian Adventure*, pp. 333f) and helped him to escape to Switzerland at the end of the war. In 1952/53 von Hentig became the first Federal German Chargé d'Affaires in Indonesia.
81 2nd edition 1979

revolvers with a plentiful supply of ammunition as well 7,000 gold coins. What a treasure! They'd never seen anything like it in Hunza. After the two Germans had confessed, there was a celebratory meal with wine, and the prisoners were allowed to consider themselves free guests. They were all suddenly getting on very well and made friends. The German major praised the unique beauty of the Hunza valley. He would have liked to remain in Karimabad, the Mir wrote in his diary.

The next day the Germans were taken to Gilgit under escort. The Mir accompanied them as far as Ganesh and bade them farewell with the wish that the Lord of the World might be merciful to them on their onward journey. They thanked him for his hospitality and the chivalry with which they had been treated in Hunza. And then all trace of them is lost. There was no more information in the Mir's diary, so we have no idea what happened to the two men and the gold – we don't even know their names.

In 1917, only a few months after the two officers passed through the Hunza Valley, the Head of the German Mission in Kabul, Werner-Otto von Hentig, set off for Hunza. Even this single rider was unable to remain concealed from British and Russian observers, and they wished to neutralise him. However, von Hentig was an old hand in the Pamir Knot and managed to keep one step ahead of his pursuers.

He had previously made a journey in 1915 from Persia to Afghanistan, which had taken him through this area. It was a struggle against Russian and British brigades as well as against thirst, dysentery and typhus. After 90 days only 37 of the 140 members actually reached their goal in Afghanistan.

In 1917, when Werner-Otto von Hentig rode out from Kabul, the First World War had made the political situation so tense that there was great suspicion, even about a single rider. The Mir of the time wrote about it in his diary, as reported by Hermann Schäfer:

Hardly had the two German officers departed, when the Mir of Hunza received a new request from the Political Agent in Gilgit, Major James, namely, to capture this single German. The Mir sent 30 Hunzakuts into the mountains to monitor crossings from Xinjiang to Hunza at the Kilik Pass. They kept watch for several days there without success. Major James now suggested moving to the village of Paik in Xinjiang, since there was a greater chance of capturing the German there. Von Hentig saw through this manoeuvre. A few days after the Hunzakuts had left the Kilik Pass, von Hentig was there with three companions looking down over the Hunza Valley at the land that belonged to the Russian and Anglo-Indian Empire. The Mir noted in his diary: how powerful must Germany be if the British Kingdom has to deploy hundreds of soldiers to deal with just one German!

Why did Great Britain, and Russia too, try with all their might to prevent Germany acquiring influence in the Pamir Knot, and why was the situation here so tense? Germany was building the Baghdad railway. The work was making massive progress and the line was pressing further and further to the east. Germany was welcomed and respected by the Turks of the Ottoman Empire. In WW1 Germany and Turkey fought together against the Allies. British and Russian distrust of everything German was particularly great, because they were afraid that a spark from the war in Western Europe might leap over to the Turkic peoples of the Pamir Knot. It was clear that they would turn against Britain and Russia and that these two great powers would thus lose their influence and hegemony in this area. The way to British India would be open and unprotected.

Von Hentig did not enter the Hunza Valley, because Britain's influence was still strong there and he could expect to be captured. He did, however, make secret contact with the Mir, who asked him to draft a constitution for his country. This he did, but we do not know how far, if at all, the draft was adopted.

The British Consul in Kashgar was extremely worried about the future of British influence in the Pamir Knot. If von Hentig succeeded in acquiring a leading role among the Turkic tribes and inciting them against the British, they would lose power in the area. At this time Kashgar was the weakest point in the region.

While the Hunzakuts went on searching for von Hentig at the Kilik Pass, he had already reached Kashgar. At this stage of World War One thousands of German and Austrian prisoners of war escaped from Russia to Xinjiang. They found a refuge in Kashgar and were granted asylum by neutral China. A further 50,000 prisoners of war were being held in Russian camps in Russian Turkestan. It was planned to free those prisoners. Macartney wrote in a report, which Hermann Schäfer found in the Mir's archives in Karimabad in the mid-1970, that von Hentig had immediately begun to agitate among the Turkic tribes. The escaped prisoners of war were on the German side anyway. The British in Kashgar were sitting on a powder keg. Revolt was in the air. The Gateway to India through the Hunza Valley was in danger of being pushed wide open. According to Macartney, von Hentig took not the slightest trouble to conceal his identity and travelled freely around Kashgar with a group of Turkmen bodyguards.

Macartney's position was weak. His career began and ended in Kashgar. He was an Eurasian with a Chinese mother. Because of the racist prejudices of the British at the time he had no chance of advancement, and because of the English blood in his veins his negotiating position vis-à-vis the Chinese was also weak.

Together with the Russians, the British attempted to get the Chinese to expel von Hentig from Xinjiang, but without success. Macartney writes that von Hentig was planning to open a German Consulate in Kashgar and that he had succeeded in setting up postal connections between Kashgar and Kabul without difficulty. There was a rumour circulating that German soldiers were already at the border.

Before the end of the war von Hentig found himself in Yarkand near the passes into the Hunza Valley. After he left Yarkand all trace of him is lost in the Chinese interior.

At the same time another German was in action in the Pamir Knot: it was Rittmeister Georg Graf von Kanitz. In 1915 he was entrusted with the mission of rousing tribes in Persia to enter the war against England on the side of the German Empire. After he had driven back the Russian army in northern Persia with the help of the native population, his next mission was to prepare war against British India. He had already made contact with the Turkmen tribes in 1910 on an expedition through the areas that were at the time Chinese Turkestan and Russian Turkestan. Now he was hunted by the Hunza Scouts on behalf of the British.

The first part of his mission was to free the approximately 40,000 Austrian and 7,000 German prisoners of war who were in camps in Russian Turkestan, and to foment uprisings against the British. Von Kanitz reported to Berlin that the prisoners of war were not properly guarded and requested money and explosives to help him realise his plans. One of these was to destroy the railway lines that the British had built in the area: he wanted his troops to be protected behind a stretch of impassable desert.

The end of the war in 1918 pre-empted the freeing of the prisoners. If this exploit had succeeded, the Gateway to India, as the Hunza Valley was known in Xinjiang, would have been wide open. After the end of the war there were about 200,000 Austrian and several thousand German prisoners of war in 40 camps in Russian Turkestan. Some of them had to remain there until 1924 as slave labourers building roads and bridges. Many died during this time, but some others founded families in the region and settled there permanently. Very little is known about this obscure war at the gates of British India. I have only been able to find three books[82] dealing with the subject.

Who were the men who hunted von Hentig and von Kanitz? They were the Hunza Scouts, a corps raised at the instigation of the British in 1912. The Mir

---

82 Paul Schaufuß, *Über den Dengis-Bei. Die abenteuerlichen Erlebnisse eines Deutschböhmen auf der Flucht vom roten Russland zum Indischen Ozean und in die Heimat* [*Over the Dengis-Bei. The adventurous experiences of a German Bohemian escaping from red Russia to the Indian Ocean and back home*, 1926; Albert O. Rust's novel *Kampf in Turkestan* [*Conflict in Turkestan*], 1934; C. P. Skrine and Pamela Nightingale, *Macartney at Kashgar: new light on British, Chinese and Russian activities in Sinkiang, 1890-1918*, 1973

of Hunza, Mohammad Nazim Tham, was to provide his best men, and the British would take over the task of training them as mountain troops, though the overall command was to remain in the hands of the Mir. Since there was no space to build barracks and training grounds in Hunza, the training was to take place in Gilgit.

The Mir sought out young men of good family. Out of 3,000 applicants he chose 500, which were then whittled down to 160. Their training lasted four weeks. The Mir himself took their oath of allegiance, and then this elite unit of former shepherds and farmers was ready. The Hunza Scouts now knew how to operate as riflemen in the high mountains and how to defeat their enemies.

When the medical officer to the British troops, McCarrison, examined the soldiers of the Hunza Scouts, he found no sign of circulatory, heart or blood vessel problems. They looked like Greek Olympic contestants, he said in admiration. He also mentioned the devastating effects of dietary problems in the West, which would only make their effects felt decades later.

Wilhelm Filchner was a German geophysicist, geodesist and explorer. He wrote over 25 popular scientific books. In 1900, at the age of 23, he had already crossed the Pamir Range on horseback. In 1903 he led an expedition to Tibet, where he was the first to undertake measurements of the earth's magnetic field. In 1911 he started on an Antarctic expedition on the ship Deutschland: The Filchner ice shelf in the Weddell Sea is named after him.

However, Filchner's first love was Central Asia, which remained his preferred field of research. At his own expense he led an expedition to the high Tibetan plateau from 1926 to 1928, making numerous geophysical measurements. His 1928 book about the expedition, 'Om mani padme hum', ran to 27 impressions.

Between 1934 and 1938 he led another expedition to Central Asia, this time financed by the German Reich. His mission was to take more magnetic measurements to link up with the measurements he had taken in 1926-1928. The area to be surveyed was to extend from the Himalayas through Xinjiang to the Pamir Range: a large part of Central Asia had not yet been surveyed.

Filchner measured, for example, the declination, inclination and intensity of the earth's magnetic field in the area, on the basis of which magnetic maps could be created to enable ships and aircraft to hold an exact course. Since Lufthansa was planning a regular flight connection to eastern China over the area surveyed by Filchner, I suspect that, like Sven Hedin, Filchner was secretly employed by the airline to make these measurements: Lufthansa's pilots would also need to be able to navigate accurately in this so-far unexplored region. Navigation by sight would be almost impossible in a desert landscape with hardly any landmarks.

To carry out the measurements, Filchner had to take extremely sensitive instruments with him, such as theodolites, a dip inductor, a magnetic field balance, torsion magnetometers and radio equipment. The measurements had to be taken at distance of 20 – or at most 30 – kilometres apart, and making one measurement took about four hours each time. In order to locate the exact spots again Filchner had to make a sketch of each site.

He began measuring in Lan-Chóu in northeast China and crossed the Gobi and Takla Makan deserts, going through marshy landscapes and salt deserts, over rubble, rough boulders and scrubby meadows. Filchner arrived in Chotan in Xinjiang in December 1936. Just outside Chotan, in Lob[83], Filchner carried out his five-hundredth measurement. He intended to travel on from Chotan via the Karakoram range to India, but things didn't turn out that way. Chotan lies on the south-western edge of the Tarim Basin and is known for its knotted carpets and bright silks.

In Chotan Filchner, as happened later to the crew of the Lufthansa aircraft D-ANOY, was arrested. He did not have a valid visa for Xinjiang. There was, moreover, a war raging, and Communist and Islamist hordes made the area unsafe. Warlords took over control in a conflict resembling a civil war, and chaos reigned. Filchner was forced to spend the winter in Chotan. Eventually, after seven months of barbarous treatment, he was released after going on hunger strike and received his passport back.

His next destination was Leh in Ladakh.[84] For Filchner, the only possible route was – as he said – the 'Route of Death' over the Karakoram. The passes he had to cross in the Himalayas and the Karakoram are impassable for eight months of the year, but now they were free of snow again. There is no evidence of which route he actually took – did he go through the Hunza Valley? It's more likely that he rode along the old caravan route over the – almost 5,600-metre – Karakoram Pass. This is somewhat to the east of the Khunjerab Pass and was the highest pass on the caravan route, thus acting as an important link between Xinjiang in China and Leh in North India. He reached Leh in September 1937, probably through the Nubra Valley, itself at an altitude of 3,000 metres. In Leh he carried out the final measurements of his 3,500-kilometre expedition.

In October 1937 he reached Srinagar in Kashmir, where he was welcomed by the German Consul General and received the first mail he had seen after years of isolation. His mission fulfilled, he returned to Germany.

---

83 Lob was where, as described above, D-ANOY made an emergency landing because of engine failure.
84 In North India

Erich von Salzmann, a Lieutenant in the Neumärkischer Field Artillery Regiment 54, had taken the same route as Filchner in 1903. He had been posted to the German garrisons in Beijing and Tientsin, and when he was demobilised he decided to return to Germany overland.

He was a good rider and had won many races, and so it is no surprise that he decided to cover the largest part of his journey to Germany on horseback. Since, unlike Filchner, he had no scientific work to do, his journey through Central Asia took far less time. Salzmann didn't go through the Hunza Valley, but he did stop in both Chotan and Kashgar. He described his experiences in his book 'Im Sattel durch Zentralasien. 6000 Kilometer in 176 Tagen' [In the Saddle Through Central Asia: 6,000 km in 176 Days].

Hunza ruled in both Chotan and Yarkand under Chinese mandate until 1912, and in the 1930s those regions were still in the sphere of influence of the Mir of Hunza. The flight of D-ANOY has already been described, since it passed along the Hunza Valley.

I have mentioned Philip Rosenthal, who visited the Hunza Valley in the 1960s in the foreword, and the travels of the explorer Sven Hedin in the 1930s in Chapter 9.

14. To Islamabad and Lahore

The flight from Gilgit to Islamabad was simply splendid. We had fantastic flying weather and a great view of K2 and then Nanga Parbat and the surrounding mountain ranges. We never stopped oohing and aahing – or photographing. But when you've taken the flight you know why good weather is absolutely necessary. Only smaller aircraft can land in Gilgit, and even the little Fokker 27 Friendship we flew in can only be loaded to 50 percent of its capacity to save weight, otherwise it would not attain the necessary altitude. It still has to fly along the valleys, because it cannot reach the altitude of Nanga Parbat. Sometimes you think the plane is almost going to touch the mountains with its wings.

Thanks to Annette's links with Annemarie Schimmel, the news of which had already reached the pilot, we were allowed to go forward to the pilot after we reached our cruising altitude and see the view from the cockpit. It was an unforgettable flight over the highest mountain massif in the world. As the captain said to us, you could see almost one hundred peaks over 7,000 metres high from here!

As we flew over the 4,173-metre Babusar Pass, one of the highest on the old caravan route, we were only a few metres above the crest of the pass. I could see the smallest details on the ground below, including the marmots, which fled to the security of their burrows.

The pilot has no margin for error here. The passes in this high mountainous area are as important for aeroplanes today as they once were for the caravans. You can easily see how such a small aircraft can disappear without trace in the mountains in bad flying weather or if there is a sudden change in the weather, as happened to the Rosinys' friend, the bookseller from Gilgit, in 1989.

Once we arrived in Islamabad, we immediately booked our flight on to Lahore. Here, too, we only had to ask an official where we could book a flight for him to call a colleague over. He was very helpful and we had soon booked the flight and checked in. And so we reached Lahore without any problems.

Here in Lahore it's quite hot – 45 °C in the shade – but that affects us less because it is a very dry heat. This afternoon we indulged in high tea in the Holiday Inn, the new hotel that had still been under construction in 1992. We were given as much coffee, cakes and snacks – sandwiches, samosas,

Ill. 120: A last look at the Hunza River ...

Ill. 121: ...and K2 from the aircraft

Ill. 122 and 123: Passing Nanga Parbat, the mountain so fateful for Germans

pakoras, pies and salads – as we could fit in. And we had a lot of room! No trace of the kind of polite restraint you would expect at such an English event as high tea. But Nemesis followed straight away. Even before we left the Holiday Inn I was stricken with severe diarrhoea. But the toilets there are so luxurious that it was a pleasure to make use of them.

In Faletti's Hotel in Lahore they were not, at the time of our visit, serving their famous high tea. Shortly after we left, the hotel, opened in 1880, was closed for restoration in the historical colonial style. It was reopened in 2013 and is now the best, most luxurious and most expensive hotel in Pakistan.

We love high tea. This English custom is actually a meal that is taken between 4 and 6 o'clock, because dinner is often eaten quite late in Britain. high tea includes among other things fruit bread, biscuits of all colours, cheese and cucumber sandwiches, muffins and cakes. Fortunately this English tea culture has survived in most former British colonies even today. For Annette and me high tea was always a must, whether we were in Pakistan, India, Burma or Singapore!

After high tea we wandered around the place a little, shaking hands with countless Pakistanis, who were full of enthusiasm for the successful A-bomb tests. We grinned at everyone until the corners of our mouths almost became fixed just below our ears and then escaped from these expressions of universal brotherhood – which get a bit exhausting after a while – back here to Faletti's Hotel. We wanted to write a bit, treat ourselves to a cool cocktail and read the paper.

Today, the 31st of May, we've looked at some of Lahore: the Badshahi Mosque, Lahore Fort, Jehangir's Tomb and of course the massive old Zam-Zama canon, cast in 1762, made world famous by Rudyard Kipling's *Kim*.

Then in the afternoon we intended to descend on the Old City, but to my great annoyance it was closed. No bazaar full of life and colour, just grey shutters, dirt and a few people who explained to us that everything is shut on Sundays. Things can't be so bad for the Pakistanis if they can afford to do this! And on a Sunday: if it had been a Friday I might have understood! Looking at an old city like this when it's all closed is really quite depressing, especially when you have such happy memories of it as I do. We'd gone there in a three-wheeled motor rickshaw, which wasn't the most pleasant experience for my back, which had been playing up again today. In spite of that we took the same mode of transport back and the driver took us through a corner of Lahore where a kind of Sunday market was taking place. That reconciled us a little to the fact that the Old City was shut.

Ill. 124: Faletti's: the old colonial hotel

Ill. 125: The Grand Mosque in Lahore

Ill. 126 and 127: In the Old City of Lahore

Ill. 128 and 129: Street kitchens on the Aabpara Market in Lahore

This evening we have filled our bellies in the Holiday Inn again, which hasn't done us – or at least me – a great deal of good. My own fault! Once again my eyes were bigger than my belly: my stomach is once more rumbling fit to burst.

Tomorrow we're off back to Islamabad, but this time by bus. We're intending to spend the last three days before our flight home there, travel to Taxila again and make some other excursions. Now I have to pack. By the way, we've realised once again that half of our luggage was superfluous. We haven't even worn everything yet! No matter how little you take with you, it's always too much.

The following day we took the bus to Rawalpindi. We were really keen, and found it much better and pleasanter than flying. The bus was very modern, clean and air-conditioned. Everyone had a reserved seat – we, as almost always, near the front – and we were handed a bag of crisps and a carton of juice as we boarded. After the bus had fought its way through the crush of traffic on the streets of Lahore, we drove off along the motorway. It had only been opened three months before, and was in no way inferior to our own autobahns.

Half way through the journey there was a break at a service station. There were a whole lot of other buses parked there, though none of them were as posh as ours. There was a motorway restaurant, and above all – loos. The men's loos were quite okay, but the women's were suffering a bit from the press of people using it. Countless women were heaving all their children onto the loo one after another, combing their hair, washing out their mouths and having a relaxed chat. The flush wasn't working in all the loos – and of course not in the one that I used. A friendly Pakistani woman waved me in after she had relieved herself. But on a journey like that you can't be too picky.

After half an hour the journey continued and after a couple of hours we arrived in Rawalpindi, fresh and completely relaxed. From the bus station we took a taxi to Islamabad. The area around the bus station seemed somehow familiar to me, and lo and behold, we'd hardly gone 500 metres in the taxi when we passed Flashman's Hotel. It looked totally unchanged from when I'd stayed there: a little down-at-heel, perhaps, but far less than Faletti's.

Flashman's was previously an elegant colonial-style hotel. Today, in 2016, it's a scruffy dump under the management of the government, where you can get both women and alcohol – you can even order a young woman and a drink from reception – in a strictly Islamic country! And in a government hotel!

And then we were back in the Ambassador Hotel, where our journey began. This time we were given a room overlooking the garden. Admittedly it was smaller than the room we'd stayed in before, but it was much quieter, brighter and nicer. The air-conditioning wasn't working properly, but although they immediately offered us another room we decided to stay in this one just because we liked it. Thank God, we don't suffer from the heat. In the evening we went for a little walk and then ate a snack in the freshly renovated dining room in the hotel. The whole hotel has been gradually renovated after new management took over in 1996.

Today, the 2nd of June, we decided to have a rest day. At 8 o'clock we had breakfast in the garden and sat there until midday. Then we slept a bit, and afterwards took a taxi to the British Airways office to confirm our flights. Then we were driven to the Hilton Hotel because we wanted to find out what the high tea there was like. We arrived at the right time, but what was on offer was not tempting enough for us to go for it. We returned to the hotel on foot, and near the bus station – not far from our Ambassador Hotel – we discovered a delightful foodie area, which we found it impossible to pass by. We bought a large portion of vegetable samosas, which were wrapped lovingly in a bag rolled out of old newspaper, and gobbled them all up on the way home. Even so, we still sat down in the garden that evening and treated ourselves to a tomato soup, a chicken corn soup and a portion of pakoras. We preferred eating out there to the dining room, even if it had been spankingly newly renovated.

Today, the 3rd of June, we visited Taxila. You can't go to Islamabad without visiting Taxila again every time. It's the cultural centre of Gandhara, and just 40 kilometres away. The first taxi-driver we approached was an unpleasant type – he seemed devious, arrogant and sleazy. He wanted 1,500 rupees for the journey and even after a lot of haggling he only went down to 1,300. So to his annoyance we approached another driver on the street, who immediately agreed to do the job for 700 rupees. The only words of English he knew were "No problem", but even though the phrase made us suspect the worst, the day went absolutely unproblematically.

Taxila is always an experience. We wandered around for hours. At every site we were offered 'genuine antique' Buddha heads – strange how they all looked exactly the same! –, old coins and other 'genuine' archaeological finds. But in fact it was all relatively restrained. In the Jaulian Monastery a camel was wandering around, and I immediately tried to make friends with it and capture the moment in a nice photo. but a local warned me that in the dry season camels could be unpleasant and aggressive and bite you. That immediately brought me to my senses, and I kept a sensible distance, always ready to flee, and in the expectation that the animal might at any moment lunge at me with a scornful grunt and bite me in the bum. I photographed it, of course, but it was by no means as picturesque as I'd hoped.

Half a dozen highly developed civilisations flourished here in the Indus Valley. The great centres of life in antiquity like Taxila or Mohenjo-daro are rich in archaeological heritage. Excavations have shown that as early as 2600 B.C. there were cultures here which built major cities with thousands of inhabitants. The cities had closely-packed large buildings of baked brick and ten-metre wide paved streets. They had covered sewage systems and seepage pits, rubbish pits, corn stores, citadels and defensive walls. For the first time in human history, baked bricks were used for all buildings. The proportions of the bricks were 1:2:4, like our modern bricks. All the houses had separate bathrooms and kitchens. The cities were planned on a rectangular grid-system.

Like Ancient Egypt and Mesopotamia, the Indus culture was one of the earliest civilisations in the world: finds have been made at more than 1,000 sites along the Indus. In the course of the excavations they have found a great number of clay pots, and on the walls of the houses and on clay tablets there are numerous characters from an as yet undeciphered script. The archaeological excavations are far from being completed, and much remains to be discovered.

Annette had previously visited Taxila and other sites of the Indus culture, like Mohenjo-daro, years before with her parents. For me, the ancient city of Taxila was unexplored territory. It lies in a beautiful valley south of the Indus north of Rawalpindi, and was the capital of the historical Gandhara empire, which flourished from 600 to 500 B.C. It was a Buddhist centre of great spiritual and cultural importance. The city lay on the trade route of the southern Silk Road which ran through the Hunza Valley. It was an important site of cultural exchange with a great university, one of the oldest in the world. There are also several monasteries in the vicinity of Taxila.

There are an impressive number of larger than life-size sculptures and many reliefs which are surprisingly similar to the masterpieces of Ancient Greece. In 326 B.C. Alexander the Great conquered the city, but his rule lasted only 9 years and ended in 317 B.C., although Hellenistic influence continued and coins of the period are still found in the Hunza Valley.

The Taxila Museum with its extraordinary collection of jewellery, coins and silver and gold vessels is most impressive. Taxila has been a UNESCO World Heritage Site since 1980.

Ill. 130 and 131: Archaeological excavations in Taxila

When we got back to the hotel later that afternoon and tried to sit down in the garden, we were informed that an event, a tea-party, was about to take place, and that we should go to the dining room instead. We had no desire at all to do that, and so we went up to our room, ordered tea there and watched what was going on from above. They set up a long table, and waiters came out with trays full of dry cakes, sandwiches and samosas. Three trays of cakes, three of sandwiches and three of samosas – so in our view as high tea connoisseurs, not the most lavish tea party. I counted a total of only 36 sandwiches! But there was something wrong with the timetable. The trays were carried out into the garden, left standing in the sun for a while and then carried back in again. Then they were brought out again and left standing in the sun once more. This was repeated at least three times.

Then all of a sudden a group of reporters arrived, recognizable by their cameras and the writing pads they took out of their briefcases. The reporters sat down to wait for what was to happen – as did we. During this whole time the gardener was impassively watering his flower-beds with a hose. The hose ran through the whole garden, and when necessary the gardener simply lifted it over the heads of the seated reporters.

Suddenly something happens: the tea-party guests arrive – all men – and the trays of culinary delights are brought out again. And look, there is immediate movement among the crowd of reporters. But it's not the guests they set upon, but the trays of snacks. They fill their plates – one of them even fills his pockets with sandwiches, another eats cake with ketchup, a third bites into a samosa, then puts it back and takes another. The garden fills up with more and more guests, some of them religious bigwigs, who do admittedly behave with a little more restraint than the reporters, but only when everything has been completely gobbled up – even the samosa with the bite out of it is eaten by a mullah holding a mobile phone in his other hand – and they're only serving tea, do the reporters remember what they've actually come to the Ambassador Hotel for, and a sort of press conference takes place. But then the meeting comes to a swift end, the tables are removed and we can take up our customary position in the garden and eat our usual evening meal of tomato soup, chicken corn soup and pakoras.

Our last day in Pakistan, the 4th of June, went just like the first: sleeping, sleeping, sleeping, lazy, lazy, lazy! There was nothing left to do but wander around a lot. We do want to make one more attempt to have high tea, and so are driven that afternoon to the best hotel in town, which used to be the

Holiday Inn, but now, I think, belongs to the Amari Hotel Group. When we arrived, we were a little too early for high tea: it's only served at a particular time, usually 4 o'clock, and that had not arrived yet, so we wandered around the shopping arcades for a while and I showed Horst the shop where I'd bought myself a lapis lazuli pendant the last time I was there. The shop owner became very active when he saw Horst and me, showing us everything he possessed. I saw the same chains there as in Karimabad, though the price was several times higher. That I had not made the best bargain possible here in 1992 – in spite of haggling – had been clear to me even at the time. The man made a great deal of effort to sell us something, but we put him off with the promise of returning a few days later, since we'd only just arrived.

In another shop we got into conversation with an Afghan. He told us about his uncle, an urologist who lives and practices in Germany. Horst immediately responded enthusiastically, because his brother has an Afghan friend of the same name in Germany who is also an urologist. This immediately made them great friends. We were given a letter to the Afghan uncle in Germany, which we gladly took with us.[85]

This Afghan also relieved me of a great burden which I had been carrying with me for the whole of our trip. He was at last able to give me the answer to a question I had been asking myself the whole time: what is the name of the valley in Afghanistan with the giant Buddha statues? Bamian, of course. It had been bothering me for weeks.

Bamian, a valley in Afghanistan at an altitude of 2,500 metres, was where the biggest standing Buddha statues of the world – up to 53 metres tall – used to be. They are said to have been created in the 6th century on the Silk Road between China and the West. There were also several Buddhist monasteries. Up to 5,000 monks lived in the numerous caves around the statues. In 2001 the statues and the majority of the caves were destroyed by the Taliban using ground-to-air artillery and explosives.[86]

After a cup of tea with the friendly Afghan we sat in the hall for a while. It boasted the statue of a rider. The whole time I thought to myself, "I know that rider, I'm sure I've seen him somewhere!", until it suddenly came to me: he looked exactly like Horst's brother Hartmut!

---

85 Note in January 1999: Horst's brother's friend was not an urologist but a proctologist, and so a different person, but we were so lost in enthusiasm that we didn't realise; we posted the letter anyway.

86 In the 1970s, when my brother Hartmut was Director of the Goethe Institute in Kabul, I was able to visit and admire the Buddha statues in the Bamian Valley with him while they were still undamaged.

And then the time had passed and we could finally proceed to our high tea, not at a run, of course, but at a slow and measured pace. When we got to the high tea, however, our behaviour was not very different from that of the reporters at the tea party, because unlike the measly high tea at the Hilton here in Islamabad, the Amari Hotel fulfilled all our expectations. There was so much on offer that it was hard to decide where to start and where to stop: with so much available you couldn't just stop because you were full!

At the next table there were two Pakistani ladies, one of whom was terribly loud, plump, self-important and gold-bedecked, accompanied by two gentlemen. The self-important lady talked almost non-stop, constantly grazing from the gentlemen's plates as well as her own; she became a sort of excuse for me to keep filling up my own plate. That evening our meal in the garden of the Ambassador Hotel was cancelled.

15. Back to Germany

Departure day! The 5th of June 1998. We were at the airport by 5:20 a.m.: we'd been told to be there four hours early when we confirmed our tickets. We thought that was wildly exaggerated, but we submitted to the rules. And, as we discovered, it was in fact absolutely necessary: check after check after check! And chaos everywhere!

First we had to stand in a horribly long queue outside the airport entrance. They checked on a list to see if we were even allowed to enter the airport, that is, had a ticket. When we finally got through this check, we were immediately standing in the next long queue: there was a baggage check. Everyone had to open everything – we too, of course. The official responsible for checking the baggage was very impatient and barked at me because I didn't have the key immediately to hand: "You don't have key?" The next thing he asked was, "Are you smoking?" I said no. The next question, "And at home?" At least that was what I understood him to be saying in his broken English, and so answered, "Also not smoking." I couldn't help laughing. Horst, to whom the questions were also addressed, understood correctly, "Your profession?" and answered, "Retired." Now the official was on the point of losing his temper and barked, "Your real profession!" He got no answer from me because I could not speak for laughing, so Horst answered, "Also retired!" At that point the official gave up checking our baggage and let us through.

But we didn't get away that quickly, because we still had to straighten out our things and shut and lock the cases again. The official became impatient and barked at us once more, "There are many people waiting! Please go!" But even that could not disturb our calm Horst, who answered extremely slowly, looking him straight in the eyes, "You asked us to open, now I have to close again! Don't rush us, Sir!" This degree of disrespect made the man speechless and we left – after the cases were locked again – with our heads held high. But that was the only unfriendly Pakistani we met on the whole trip.

Next we were allowed to check in, then came passport control, then the security check where everything we had with us had to be opened again – and our passports checked once more. Many Pakistanis had their hand baggage pierced through with giant needles. And then more passport checks – this was the seventh time! Then once more as we left the airport building, and another time before we were allowed to board the plane. With so many checks we felt quite safe on this British Airways flight.

There was an hour's delay, and when we finally took off it was after 9 o'clock. At least five PIA flights had been cancelled that morning, including one to London, so the passengers from that were crammed into our British Airways Boeing 747-400: every last seat was taken! Masses of howling children – one of them quite close to us howled for practically the whole ten-hour journey. Its mother kept fainting! Any trace of love for children went straight out of the window – not only mine, but that of the Pakistanis around us. The flight itself, however, compensated us for the level of noise. It was good, clear flying weather, and we saw the highest mountains of the world laid out beneath us one more time. The weather remained fine all the way to England, so that we had wonderful views to look down on the whole time and so were able – in spite of the screeching child – to enjoy the flight.

On landing in Manchester, we went immediately to our old place of refuge behind the pillar at gate 23. We did, after all, have a wait of several hours, which we spent in deep sleep – and luckily, our onward flight left from that very gate.

Shortly before our departure Horst provoked an English-speaking fellow-passenger who insisted on holding a conversation on his mobile at the top of his voice in the middle of the crowd. No one could help hearing the conversation. The caller got the person he was talking to to dictate a phone number to him, which he repeated very loudly several times: Horst had by now had more than enough and decided to intervene. He began to shout numbers out equally loudly – but different ones from the ones the man was reciting. This confused him totally, and he couldn't remember the phone number he was being given. He abused Horst most aggressively, and would probably have liked to punch him, but since all the other passengers were applauding Horst's action he probably didn't have the nerve to do anything more. That was our last good deed on English soil – and then we set off for home.

After a good hour's flight from Manchester to Köln/Bonn airport we were back, safe and sound, if a little melancholic, in Germany. Our lovely, eventful and interesting trip was now consigned to memory. When a journey has been as beautiful and exciting as this one, you never want it to stop! Admittedly, we did say during our preparations that this was surely a once in a lifetime experience, but today it already seems to us that we will travel to the Hunza Valley once more.

Closing remark, We didn't manage a return journey to the Hunza Valley, and today, 18 years later, a holiday in Pakistan, even in the peaceful Hunza Valley, has become far too dangerous.

16. The Karakoram Highway and the Hunza Valley 2015/2016

18 years have passed since our journey along the KKH through the Hunza Valley to Kashgar. During that time the Hunza Valley and Xinjiang have attracted ever more attention and interest from the tourist industry. In the 1970s it seemed almost impossible, for reasons of the travel infrastructure alone, to visit these areas. And rightly, because the journey implied all kinds of difficulties which required a great deal of physical effort and a willingness to do without those comforts which the tourist has become accustomed to find everywhere in the world. Until then, travelling in these regions was a privilege reserved for explorers, diplomats, mountain climbers and a few adventurers.

I kept asking myself what it looks like there now. Was it still possible to drive along the KKH? In 1998 Annette and I doubted whether it would still be possible to do so in 20 years' time. At the beginning of this year I had the opportunity to talk to my old Pakistani fellow-student, who as an engineer is very interested in the KKH and receives regular information about the state of the road.

Today we hear very little positive news from Pakistan, but the Hunza Valley is still the safest area. Nevertheless, Western tourists have stayed away since 2001 because of the tense political situation. Pakistan has simply become too dangerous as a travel destination.

In 2013 there was a further setback. This time the cause was not the murderous Nanga Parbat, but the bloodthirsty Taliban. Shortly after the beginning of the climbing season, members of the Taliban disguised in military police uniforms attacked eleven climbers by night and murdered them. Until then this area had been free of terrorist actions. Three Chinese, four Ukrainians, a Russian, a Lithuanian, a Nepalese and the Pakistani mountain guide were the victims. For the Taliban, all foreigners are enemies. After this massacre in what had until then been classed as a safe area, climbing tourism has come to a complete halt.

When Annette and I travelled the KKH, photographing bridges was already prohibited, but at the time nobody checked. For me as an engineer the suspension bridges were simply technically interesting constructions, and it didn't disturb even members of the military if I photographed a bridge. They say it is different now! The KKH is under strict surveillance, and if you are caught, the penalties are high. You also lose your flash card, or even your whole camera.

The KKH is still closed in winter and is impassable for a few months. In parts of the Hunza Valley the road is still just a gravel track and a permanent construc-

tion site. The Chinese government has made 400 million US dollars available for expanding the road to two, and in some places even four, asphalt lanes. Massive walls will be built to protect against landslides and rock falls. At especially dangerous spots the road is to be diverted into tunnels carved out of the cliffs. There is also supposed to be a gas pipeline running parallel to the KKH. The work is supposed to be completed in 2019: all made possible by China!

As I have already said, there was a massive landslide near Attabad on the 4th of January 2010 which blocked the Hunza River. An avalanche of boulders swept down from a height of 1,500 metres above the river and came to a halt at a height of 200 metres on the other side. This was only 18 kilometres north of Karimabad, quite close to the landslide that nearly buried Annette and me in 1998, and blocked the Hunza River, creating the 27 kilometre long Lake Attabad, which now reaches as far as Gulmit. Anyone who wants to travel northwards to the Khunjerab Pass now has to take a simple ferry over the lake, which is 100 metres deep in places.

Twenty people were buried under the landslide and five villages were inundated. Several thousand people had to be evacuated. 25 kilometres of the KKH were destroyed or lay 30 metres below the surface of the water. Six suspension bridges were swept away. The lower Shishkal Valley, which I tried to reach over the dangerous traditional bridge near Gulmit, was completely flooded, as was the bridge, of course.

Almost 40 percent of the village of Gulmit, which we loved so much, and where we spent several days on both legs of our journey, was flooded, and it could initially only be reached by boat. The Hunza Marco Polo Inn was not affected by the flooding since it is built on a hill above the village. Since then it has even been extended by a new modern wing, as they expect the lake to be a new tourist attraction. But unfortunately the tourists are still staying away because of the uncertain political situation.

To get around the new lake, a new 24-kilometre stretch of the KKH was built at a higher level with viaducts and five tunnels and opened in September 2015. The tunnels bored through the rock by the Chinese have a total length of 7 kilometres. This diversion cost $ 275 million. China is not afraid of expense!

The KKH is of great strategic importance to China. Even though the exchange of goods between China and Pakistan on the KKH is not very extensive at the moment, China is expecting a massive increase in the future. Large containers will be transported along the KKH to the port of Karachi.

Since the stability of the dam created by the landslide is uncertain, about 15,000 people in 36 villages down river are in great danger. In the worst case scenario a tidal wave 18 metres high is predicted.

On the border between Pakistan and China at the Khunjerab Pass, China has built a massive new border station, in the style of a castle. When Annette and I crossed it, the Chinese border officials were still living in simple caravans and containers.

Since the KKH over the Khunjerab Pass was opened to traffic, the Mingteke and Kilik passes have lost their importance. These remote passes in the Hunza Valley are now only used by the occasional smuggler. Commercial traffic from Xinjiang through the valley to northern Pakistan now only flows over the Khunjerab Pass. The long caravans have been replaced by columns of lorries.

In Xinjiang the rights of the ethnic minorities, like the Uyghurs and Kirghiz, have been further restricted. In Kashgar, Han Chinese are allowed to fill 20-litre fuel cans, but this is prohibited to the ethnic minorities for security reasons. They are also forbidden to carry pocket knives or large quantities of matches. Even the way the women veil themselves is subject to regulation. The list goes on and on. Stop and search, harassment, humiliation on the streets are the order of the day. No wonder the minorities are constantly rebelling against this oppression.

The Hunzakuts don't have these problems. They are able to live in their lovely valley without too much interference from the Pakistani government. When we were there we met nothing but friendly, helpful and hospitable people.

But why was the attitude of the Hunzakuts towards the British so reserved, not to say unfriendly, at the time of our visit? Was it still the effects of the wars at the end of the 19th century, when the Hunza Valley was conquered by force by the British and the King of Hunza deposed? As we have seen there was very close co-operation with the successor appointed by the British, Mir Mohammad Nazim Tham. And British explorers helped to open up the country. But to this very day the Hunzakuts are apparently unable to forget British interference in their affairs in the past.

    As my Pakistani friend observes, hostility to the USA and Britain has been on the increase as a consequence of the wars they have waged in Iraq and Afghanistan. Because of the wars unleashed in neighbouring countries, the whole region has been destabilised and Pakistan has been particularly hard hit economically. Even the tolerant Hunzakuts mention with some bitterness the fact that tourism has collapsed as a result of these wars. The hotels stand empty. Previously, they say, there were no Taliban and no Islamic State. These terror organisations arose initially in response to the wars waged totally in contravention of international law by the USA and Britain.

The beautiful Hunza Valley survived peacefully for centuries in complete isolation from outside influences. The inhabitants had to struggle for existence and survival every day. Nevertheless, they were satisfied. The KKH and the wars in the region have seriously altered Hunzakut life. We can only hope that peace will one day return to the region, and that the Hunzakuts will be able to maintain the life-style to which they have been accustomed for centuries in peace. But perhaps that is just wishful thinking. The world is changing everywhere – and nowhere more than in the Hunza Valley.

17. Thanks

At the end of this book I would firstly like to give especial posthumous thanks to Annette. Her travel reports and witty comments laid the foundations of this book. She was also always an ideal and loyal travelling companion, who went through thick and thin all over the world with me without a word of complaint, even in the most difficult of situations.

I would also like to thank her father, the orientalist Professor Hans Bräker, who died far too early. As an expert on Central Asia he helped bring me closer to the Xinjiang region during hours of discussion and conversation.

Thanks, too, to my brother Hartmut, who told me about many details of his earlier visit to the Hunza Valley and read through my manuscript.

Heartfelt thanks, too, to my dear friend of many years, Michaela Mattern, who very kindly proofread my first draft.

A thousand thanks too to the many people from the Hunza Valley and Xinjiang, who told me in countless friendly conversations about their homelands and provided important information about cuisine, cultures, customs, language and history.

Especial thanks are due to those men and women who offered us a helping hand in moments of danger.

Autumn/Winter 2016/17
Horst H. Geerken

Ill. 132 and 133: Photographs of rock-drawings taken by H. Bräker in 1976.[87]

87 The illustrations were kindly placed at my disposal by Ilse Bräker, © Ilse Bräker

Ill. 134 and 135: Photographs of rock-drawings taken by H. Bräker in 1976.[88]

---

[88] The illustrations were kindly placed at my disposal by Ilse Bräker, © Ilse Bräker

18. Literature

Amin, Mohamed; Willetts, Duncan; Hancock, Graham, *Reise durch Pakistan,* 1990
Bauer, Paul, *Auf Kundfahrt im Himalaya,* 1937
Brentjes, Burchard, *Der Knoten Asiens,* 1983
Brescius, Moritz von and Kaiser, Friederike, *Über den Himalaya. Die Expeditionen der Brüder Schlagintweit nach Indien und Zentralasien 1854-1858,* 2015
Deutsche Himalaya Stiftung, *Nanga Parbat,* 1943
Dun, Mao, *Seidenraupen im Frühling,* 1987
Durand, Algernon, *The Marking of a Frontier,* 1899
Filchner, Wilhelm, *Vom Huang-Ho zum Indus,* 1969
Finsterwald, Richard, *Forschung am Nanga Parbat,* 1935
Gablenz, Carl August Freiherr von, *D-Anoy bezwingt den Pamir,* 1937
Hedin, Sven, *Durch Asiens Wüsten,* 1949
Hedin, Sven, *Transhimalaya,* 1909
Hentig, Werner-Otto von, *Mein Leben eine Dienstreise,* 1960
Hentig, Werner-Otto von, *Meine Diplomatenreise ins verschlossene Land,* 1918
Hentig, Werner-Otto von, *Von Kabul nach Shanghai,* 2003
Hoffmann-Loss, Herbert, *Bericht über eine Reise in das Gebiet des nördlichen Hindukusch,* 1977
Hopkirk, Peter, *The Great Game,* 1994
Hughes, Thomas L., *The German Mission in Afghanistan, 1914-1916,* 2004
Kanitz, G.K.E. von, *Bericht über eine Reise nach Russisch-Turkestan,* 1910
Klimkeit, Hans-Joachim, *Die Seidenstraße,* 1988
Knight, E.F., *Where Three Empires Meet,* 1900
Leitner, G.W., *Dardistan, The Hunza and Nagyr Handbook,* First reprint 1978
Lorimer, D.L.R., *The Supernatural in the Popular Belief of the Gilgit Religion,* 1929
Marshall, Alex, *The Russian General Staff and Asia, 1860-1917*
Müller-Stellrecht, Irmtraud, *Hunza und China,* 1978
Polo, Marco, *The Travels,* translated by Nigel Cliff, Penguin Classics 2015
Rust, Albert O., *Kampf in Turkestan,* 1934
Salzmann, Erich von, *Im Sattel durch Zentralasien,* 1903
Schäfer, Hermann, *Hunza,* 1979
Schimmel, Annemarie, *Pakistan – ein Schloss mit tausend Toren,* 1965

Seidt, Hans-Ulrich, *Berlin, Kabul, Moskau. Oskar Ritter von Niedermayer und Deutschlands Geopolitik,* 2002
Shipton, Eric, *Mountain of Tartary,* 1953
Skrine, C. P. and Pamela Nightingale, *Macartney at Kashgar: new light on British, Chinese and Russian activities in Sinkiang, 1890-1918,* 1973
Taylor, Renée, *Die Gesundheits-Geheimnisse der Hunza,* 1982
Thubron, Colin, *Im Schatten der Seidenstraße,* 2013
Timmermann, Irmgard, *Die Seide Chinas,* 1986
Younghusband, Francis, *The Heart of a Continent,* 1904

19. Index of Persons

Abdullah Baig   10, 36, 39, 41, 43ff, 49f, 52, 167, 181
Aga Khan   10, 12, 52, 54, 57f, 70, 73, 170
Aga Khan IV, Karim   54, 57
Alexander Iskandar Shah   7
Alexander the Great   7, 60, 193, 212
Aly Khan   54, 57
Aufschnaiter, Peter   32
Bauer, Paul   32
Berger. Herrmann   62
Biddulph, John   193
Bircher, Ralf   176
Bräker, Prof. Hans   12f, 48, 126, 135, 223ff
Buhl, Hermann   32
Chamberlain, Colonel   193f
Curzon, Lord George   193ff
Genghis Khan   133
Durand, Algernon George Arnold   8, 63, 226
Filchner, Wilhelm   117f, 200ff, 226
Finsterwald, Richard   226
Fleming, Peter   118
Gablenz, August Freiherr von   117f, 226
Geerken, Hartmut   10ff, 33, 165, 187ff, 215, 223
German, Mr.   11f, 187-190
Glasenapp, Prof. Helmut von   12
Harrer, Heinrich   32
Hedin, Sven   104, 115, 117ff, 200, 202, 226
Hentig, Werner-Otto von   196-199, 226
Herrligkoffer, Karl Maria   32f
Herodotus   7
Hilton, James   9, 89, 183, 188
Hoffmann-Loss, Herbert   226
Hohenzollern, Waldemar Prinz von   193
Hopkirk, Peter   226
Hughes, Thomas L.   226
Humboldt, Alexander von   133, 135, 193
Ikram E. Beg   188
James, Major   196f
Kanitz, Georg Graf von   199, 226
King George V   195
Kitchener, Lord Herbert   195
Klimkeit, Prof. Hans-Joachim   12, 226
Leitner, Dr Gottlieb Wilhelm   7, 63, 65, 193, 226
Lorimer, David Lockhart Robertson   193, 226
Macartney, George   196, 198f, 227
Mao Zedong   136, 141
Marco Polo   66f, 133, 193, 226
Marshall, Alex   137, 226
McCarrison, Dr   200
Merkel, Willi   30, 32
Messner, Reinhold   32
Minto, Earl of   195
Mir Gazanfar Ali   58
Mir Mohammad Nazim Tham   58, 66, 193, 200, 221
Mir Muhammad Jamal Khan   11f, 170
Mir Safdar Ali   8, 65f
Mohammed Amin al Husseini   196
Müller-Stellrecht, Irmtraud   226

Mummery, Alfred 30
Peri 30, 62, 134
Qazim Beg 194
Raja Bahadur Khan 167, 169
Raja Hussein Khan 92, 96, 165, 167ff, 171, 188
Rosenthal, Philip 10, 202
Rosiny, Tonny 15ff, 41, 52, 84, 90, 93, 167, 182f, 203
Rust, Albert O. 199, 226
Schäfer, Hermann 196ff, 226
Schaufuß, Paul 199
Schimmel, Annemarie 191f, 203, 226
Schlagintweit, Adolf 104, 133ff, 156, 193, 226
Seidt, Hans-Ulrich 227
Shah Khan 93, 96, 167
Shaw, Robert 135
Sheng Shitsai 136
Shipton, Eric 60, 227
Sultan Mohammed Aga Khan III 57
Thoenes, Lex 32
Timur Lenk 133
Wien, Karl 30
Yaqub Beg 125, 133, 135
Younghusband, Francis 227

20. Subject Index

Afghanistan 6, 7, 9f, 10, 13, 36, 69, 98, 117, 124, 137, 194f, 197, 215, 221, 226
All India Muslim League 57
Altit 44, 58, 60f, 66, 73ff
Attabad 36, 220
Babusar Pass 20, 22, 29, 34, 203
Baghdad Railway 137, 195, 198
Baltit 11, 34, 54, 58, 60, 62f, 66, 70, 73, 179, 196
Bamian 215
Besham 22, 25, 27
Bopao Festival 57f
Burushaski 7, 62, 143, 193
Chilas 19f, 22, 29f, 34
Chitral 8, 189, 194
Chotan 117f, 185, 201f
Consulate 127f, 135f, 198
D-ANOY 117f, 201f, 226
Dasu 19, 22ff, 27ff, 34, 76, 165
Dehra Dun 32
Dras 125
Earth's magnetic field 200f
Fairy Meadows 10, 30f, 33
Gandhara 15, 49, 211f
Ganesh 44, 58, 76ff, 83, 97, 197
Gangtok 125
Gulmit 10, 29, 57, 73, 84-91, 93-96, 98, 100, 102, 148, 156, 161, 165ff, 169ff, 173, 177, 181, 188f, 220
Harappa 15, 67
high tea 203, 206, 211, 214ff
Hopar 44, 77-80, 82ff, 87, 140
Hunza Scouts 66, 199f
Hussainabad 41, 43f, 50-53

Indonesia 69, 73, 135, 196
Jaglot 36
Jalalabad 194
Junkers Ju 52 32, 117f
Kabul 6, 10, 66, 117f, 195-198, 215, 226f
Kamaris 171
Karakoram Pass 201
Karakul Lake 114ff, 119 151, 170
Kashmir 6, 7, 32, 54, 65, 118, 125, 193, 201
Khunjerab Pass 6, 33, 67, 96, 98f, 102, 107, 124, 134, 148, 160f, 169, 194, 201, 220f
Kilik Pass 67, 98, 107, 194f, 197f, 221
Ladakh 33, 58, 98, 102, 113, 125, 201
Lan-Chóu 201
Leh 102, 125, 201
Lhasa 70, 148
Line of Control, LOC 125
Lowari Tunnel 194
Lufthansa 54, 115, 200f
Manshera 20
Mingteke Pass 67, 98, 107, 194ff, 221
Misgar 195
Mohenjo-daro 67, 212
Nanga Parbat 6, 10, 20, 30-35, 118, 134, 191, 203, 205, 219, 226
Nathula-La Pass 125
Nubra Valley 201
Nuristan 194
Passu 57, 97f, 170, 196
Peshawar 6, 66

PIA   184, 191f, 218
Polo   9, 57f, 70, 96, 182
Rakaposhi   7, 34, 44, 58, 71, 173
Rawalpindi   10, 22, 24, 36, 124, 210, 212
Recipes   149f, 174f
Rock drawings   33, 45-49, 224f
Shangri La   9, 89, 188
Shishkat   88f, 97f
Sikkim   125
Skardu   35
Srinagar   6, 32, 201
Sust   93, 97f, 101f, 106f, 112f, 119, 127, 129, 148, 151, 161, 169
Takla Makan   68f, 115, 117f, 122, 155, 201
Taliban   32, 215, 219, 222
Tarim Basin   114f, 195f, 201
Taxila   20, 22, 66f, 210-213
Thakot   22
The Great Game   13ff, 65, 135ff, 226
Tibet   13, 33, 58, 62, 113, 124f, 148, 200
Tirich Mir   35
Ultar Glacier   44, 71
Ürümqi   124, 148
Wakhan   194
Wine   10, 69ff, 178f, 185, 197
Xian   67, 117
Yarkand   63, 67, 117f, 134f, 199, 202

Some words which appear very frequently in the book have not been included in the subject index, for example:
Gilgit
Himalaya
Hindu Kush
Hunza
Indus
Karakorama
Karimabad
Kashgar
Nagar
Pamir
Tashkurgan
Xinjiang

Further Books by the Author

Horst H. Geerken
Der Ruf des Geckos. 18 erlebnisreiche Jahre in Indonesien
436 Seiten, Paperback, Norderstedt 2009
ISBN 978-3-8391-1040-9, EUR 24,90

Horst H. Geerken
A Gecko for Luck. 18 years in Indonesia
392 Pages, Paperback, Norderstedt 2010
ISBN 978-3-8391-5248-5, EUR 24,95

Horst H. Geerken
A Magic Gecko. CIA's Role Behind the Fall of Soekarno
360 Pages, Paperback, Jakarta 2011
ISBN 978-979-709-554-3, IRP 150.000,00

Horst H. Geerken
A Magic Gecko. Peran CIA di Balik Jatuhnya Soekarno
498 Pages, Paperback, Jakarta 2011
ISBN 978-979-709-555-0, IRP 85.000,00

Horst H. Geerken
Missbrauchte Kindheit. Geboren im Jahr von Hitlers Machtergreifung
240 Seiten, Paperback, Norderstedt 2011
ISBN 978-3-8423-4909-4, EUR 16,90

Horst H. Geerken
Hitlers Griff nach Asien, Band 1
380 Seiten, Paperback, Norderstedt 2015
ISBN 978-3-7347-4291-0, EUR 27,95

Horst H. Geerken
Hitlers Griff nach Asien, Band 2
432 Seiten, Paperback, Norderstedt 2015
ISBN 978-3-7347-4293-4, EUR 27,95

Horst H. Geerken
Hitler's Asian Adventure
572 Seiten, Paperback, Norderstedt 2015
ISBN 978-3-7386-3013-8, EUR 27,95

Annette Bräker, Horst H. Geerken
Indonesien, Gestern und Heute. Reiseberichte der anderen Art
316 Seiten, Paperback, Norderstedt 2016
ISBN 978-3-7392-0909-8, € 19,95

Horst H. Geerken
Jejak Hitler di Indonesia
402 Seiten, Paperback, Jakarta 2017
ISBN 978-602-412-175-4, IRP 119.000,00

All these books are also available as e-book/Kindle editions
BukitCinta Books
www.bukitcinta.com